More five-minute writing

More five-minute writing

Another 50 inspiring exercises in creative writing in ~~five~~ minutes a day

Margret Geraghty

howtobooks

Constable & Robinson Ltd
55–56 Russell Square
London WC1B 4HP
www.constablerobinson.com

First published in the UK by How To Books,
an imprint of Constable & Robinson Ltd, 2013

© 2013 Margret Geraghty

The right of Margret Geraghty to be identified as the author of this
work has been asserted by her in accordance with the
Copyright, Designs and Patents Act 1988

A copy of the British Library Cataloguing in
Publication Data is available from the British Library

ISBN 978-1-84528-509-8

Printed and bound in the UK

1 3 5 7 9 10 8 6 4 2

Contents

Introduction

On a warm summer day in 2007, I resigned from teaching in adult education. I loved my writing classes but not the growing mound of administrative paperwork. When one of the office staff revealed that none of this paperwork was ever read but was just filed to comply with regulations, I decided that enough was enough. I wanted to teach, not fill in forms, particularly those that asked me to rate a student's learning on a scale of one to five.

There was just one problem. The students didn't want to stop. They found a new place to meet and asked me to continue. And so Valley Writers – named after that first venue – was born. Every Monday evening, 12 of us crowded into a small room, to discuss fiction and how to write it. The room was a bit stuffy and we would often hear blood-curdling battle cries from the martial art session along the hall, but that didn't matter. We were free to do whatever we wanted. In one memorable session intended to raise awareness of textures, we played blind man's buff, but with a twist. Half the students acted as guides, leading their partners to touch different surfaces, including trees, walls and – according to one student but denied by her guide – 'road kill'.

The sessions were fun. They were experimental, both for me and the students, who often did not know what next week would bring. One feature, however, remained inviolate. The five-minute exercise. In all my years of teaching, I've never come across a writer who disliked these short bursts of writing. That doesn't mean that every exercise is equally helpful. Rather, it means that working quickly taps the unconscious in a way that often surprises the writers themselves. 'I don't know where that came from' is a common response when the time is up. John Steinbeck once articulated the process well in an interview with the *Paris Review*.

> *Write freely and as rapidly as possible and throw the whole thing on paper. Never correct or rewrite until the whole thing is down. Rewrite in process is usually found to be an excuse for not going on. It also interferes with flow and rhythm which can only come from a kind of unconscious association with the material.*

The five-minute exercise is not about producing a perfect piece of work – if indeed such a thing exists. It's about inspiration, exploration, and – most important of all – freedom.

I had to leave Valley Writers behind when I moved to the Cotswolds. The sessions live on in the pages of this book, for which I've selected the best of our exercises. There are plenty of brand-new exercises, too, inspired by topical stories and fresh research. That's the thing about writing. Our source material is like the sea: always there, but constantly changing. I've also included a new feature, Snippet Triggers, designed to show you how to develop stories from those quirky little anecdotes you find in newspapers, magazines and on the Internet. One of my own first successes was triggered by something I read in a newspaper and I know that other writers are similarly inspired.

This book is for you. I hope you will enjoy doing these exercises as much as I have enjoyed writing them. Dip in today.

Scintillating Sentences

Have you ever felt you'd like to be a touch more poetic in your writing? Perhaps you recall certain poems from your childhood but are not sure what makes them so memorable. Or maybe you're not interested in poetry at all but just want to tap into its rich use of language.

Well, for starters, take another look at the humble tongue twister. As children, we all fell about laughing as we tried to get to grips with *She Sells Seashells by the Seashore* or *Peter Piper Picked a Peck of Pickled Pepper*. But the tongue twister is just one example of a literary device called alliteration, the effect created when two or more words with the same initial sound are used close together. In poetry, William Blake's *Tyger, tyger, burning bright* is a simple but classic example. Try replacing *burning bright* with another phrase. *Tiger, tiger, flaming bright* just doesn't cut it. Neither does, *Tiger, tiger, burning gold.* It's the repeated 'b' sound that works the magic.

Here are some other poetic examples to whet your appetite:

Fly o'er waste fens and windy fields.

Alfred Tennyson, *Sir Galahad*

Deep into that darkness peering, long I stood there wondering, fearing,

Doubting, dreaming dreams no mortal ever dared to dream before;

Edgar Allan Poe, *The Raven*

And each slow dusk a drawing-down of blinds.

Wilfrid Owen, *Anthem for Doomed Youth*

But let's not get stuck on poetry. Alliteration is a versatile technique that works for many different types of writing. Ad agencies use it to create memorable slogans such as *You'll never put a better bit of butter on your knife.* Copy-editors use it to create catchy headlines: *Birthday girl Kate looks lovely in lace.* Even government departments get in on the act. Remember *Don't drink and drive?*

Alliteration is also a favourite with great orators. In 47 BCE, Julius Caesar shouted 'Veni, vidi, vici' after his overthrow of a rebellious king. In 1961, John F. Kennedy's inaugural address urged the American people to 'Let us go forth to lead the land we love.' More recently, Barack Obama told an awed audience that 'Our campaign was not hatched in the halls of Washington – it began in the backyards of Des Moines and the living rooms of Concord and the front porches of Charleston'.

For straightforward prose, the trick is not to overdo it or the impact will be lost. Amely Greeven writes about fashion, preventive health care and the mind–body–spirit balance. See how she uses alliteration to highlight the moment she decided to leave her life in the city and move to a log cabin in Jackson Hole, Wyoming:

For a second, sparkly city things danced like sugarplums in my head: salsa music on street corners, lofts with poured-

concrete floors, kisses in cabs after cocktails. But I was pretty sure I couldn't sacrifice the aliveness I felt for that familiar lifestyle.

That first sentence is a goody-bag of alliteration which helps to create a lyrical quality. Note how the soft 's' sounds at the beginning contrast with the harder 'c' sounds at the end. In the second sentence, by contrast, it's far less obvious. The result is a piece that tweaks the senses but doesn't overwhelm.

Consider using alliteration whenever you want to enhance sensory impact or elicit emotion. This is particularly useful when you want to set a scene without overloading the reader with descriptive detail:

Skeletal birch trees rise from the snow-covered ground against a backdrop of cloud-heavy skies and white mountains.

That sentence is from the introductory paragraph of an article by Alice Westgate in *Homes and Gardens* magazine. The rest of the piece is quite factual, describing how a couple built their own ski lodge in Sweden. The author's careful use of alliteration sets the scene beautifully and gives the opening an emotive quality it might otherwise lack.

THE EXERCISE

To help stimulate alliterative thinking, construct sentences in which most of the words start with the same initial sound. Remember that it's the sound that counts, not the letter. A soft 'c' – as in city – sounds like 's' whereas a hard 'c' – as in cat – sounds like 'k'.

Have fun with your sentences and don't worry if they don't make great sense.

Start with short ones until you've got the hang of it. You can then move on to longer more elaborate ones, even a complete poem if you like. Feel free to experiment, maybe using a different sound for each line or mixing two sounds in the same line as Tennyson does in *Sir Galahad*. Warning: this is addictive!

Here are some examples to get you started.

◆ Daisy dries dinner dishes in the doorway to the dismal dining room.

◆ The boisterous boy bounces into the Bertinet Bakery to buy a baguette.

◆ The lonely llama lollops through the lilacs and into the library to look for liquorice.

◆ Katie craved a cup of coffee in Karachi but could not catch a cab.

◆ Six smiling sailors swaggered down the street, sucking spearmint syrup through sticky silver straws.

◆ The crazy cat cartwheeled over the caramel cupcake before crashing into the corner cupboard.

2

Snippet Trigger – Who Did That?

I love those quirky little stories that appear in the snippets section of newspapers and the tale end of regional broadcasts. My own magazine fiction was often inspired by reading such pieces and I'm not alone. When best-selling novelist Wendy Holden was asked where she gets her ideas, she replied: 'Everywhere. But a lot come from newspapers.' Throughout this book, I've included a few of these snippet triggers. They need little introduction except the facts. Here's one to get you thinking.

A Qantas Boeing 767 aircraft was flying from Darwin to Brisbane when passengers complained about fumes in the cabin. The pilot, following standard procedure, aborted the flight and brought the plane down in Mount Isa. Unfortunately, Mount Isa is 1,500 miles from Brisbane and has no stairs suitable for disembarking such a large plane. The passengers had to be taken off by forklift – five at a time. It took two hours, after which the journey continued on another plane but without the luggage, which was still on the first plane. OMG, as they say on Twitter. The fumes were eventually traced to a dirty nappy stuffed down the aircraft's loo.

My immediate thought was: Did the nappy-stuffer own up? And my second: How awful to be responsible for wasting so many people's time, costing the airline goodness knows how much money, and being – well, a bit stupid. But then, haven't we all done silly things in our time? Haven't we all wished we'd thought about the consequences *before,* instead of after, the effect?

Sometimes, it's not even lack of thought but too much thought. For example, I like to switch off wall-sockets when I'm not using them. I once switched off what I thought was the kettle in someone else's house. It was the freezer. Similarly, the manager of my favourite local pub once thought it would be a good idea to recycle the Christmas tree on the pub's lovely open fire. Unfortunately, he didn't know his trees. This one was a Norwegian Spruce, which sparks badly and burns very hot. Within minutes the chimney was ablaze. The fire brigade arrived just in time to stop the flames shooting sideways under the ancient upstairs floorboards and burning down the building.

Fiction thrives on this kind of domino effect. To take just one example, in the film *Meet the Parents*, Greg is hoping to impress his fiancée's parents during his first visit to their home. Desperate for a smoke but knowing that his future father-in-law disapproves, he slips out onto the roof to light up. When the family cat appears, Greg drops the cigarette, which promptly rolls into the gutter and ignites some dry leaves. As Greg frantically tries to stamp out the flames, the gutter snaps and tears into a power line, which also ignites, sending a path of flame across the lawn into a collection of garden furniture and a beautiful gazebo that's been hand-carved from a single piece of wood as a wedding present for Greg's girlfriend's sister.

It's one of the funniest scenes in the film, mainly because it's the kind of awful thing that could happen to anyone and we're just glad it's not us. Greg, of course, instinctively does a runner like a naughty child, and that, in turn, takes us back to childhood and our own misdemeanours.

Which brings me back to my first thought about the Qantas incident. Did the person who put the nappy down the loo own up? It's a tough call. It's one thing to know you've been silly but when everyone else knows it, too, you feel a fool. But if you don't own up and you're found out, that's even worse. Now you're not just a fool but a coward, too. This is a topic well worth exploring. Try the following exercise.

THE EXERCISE

Do a five-minute freewrite using 'Owning up' as your trigger. Remember that with freewriting it's best if you don't think too hard about the topic. Just start writing without worrying about shape, structure, or even grammar.

3

The Nostalgic Tastebud

Waitrose Kitchen[1] magazine once invited several authors to talk about the family stories evoked by cooking and the power of shared family recipes to link the generations. The memories were fascinating. For Pulitzer Prize-winning journalist Matt McAllester, oeufs en cocotte, served in 'little brown cauldron things', always remind him of his mother, a lifelong fan of Elizabeth David. When his mother died, he had been 'pole-axed by grief and needed a coping mechanism; cooking some of her favourite recipes seemed to be it'.

For Miranda Gardiner, a keen cook since the age of five, a recipe for flapjack brought her closer to her father. It even led to a book, *Teaching Dad to Cook Flapjack*: 'Dad wanted something sweet to go with his afternoon cup of tea, and Mum used to make flapjack a lot.' It was, she says, a good recipe to teach him over the phone as he didn't have to use scales. All the ingredients could be measured in cups.

Even if we're not cooks ourselves, we all remember certain tastes and flavours of the past. Those memories act as triggers for our personal stories. For example, my husband has vivid memories of his grandmother serving Libby's sliced tinned peaches as a weekend treat. Similarly, I recall being taught to toast marshmallows by an American girl whose family had relocated to

---

1   'Nostalgia on a Plate', Waitrose Kitchen, June 2010, pp. 52–8.

Dublin where I was at school. She was from Minnesota, an impossibly glamorous and faraway place where the houses had yards instead of gardens and children were allowed to chew gum without being slapped.

L. P. Hartley was right – the past is indeed a foreign country. But the past can shape the future in surprising ways. My passion for toasted marshmallows led to an interest in American culture and, in particular, American Western films. We didn't have academic Film Studies courses when I was 18, but when they eventually arrived I was first in the queue.

Now it's your turn. Try the following exercise.

THE EXERCISE

Make a list of your own tastes and flavours of the past. If you have shared family recipes, that's great. If not, don't worry. Just think about the edible things that have special meaning for you because of the people you were close to at the time. When you've done that, choose one memory to explore in more detail and write for five minutes.

Note: For another exercise involving food, try Exercise 25 in 'We Are What We Eat'.

4

Breaking the Link

I'll let you into a secret. I've always hated working out: all those
repetitions, all that stretching, all that trying to do better than I
did on my last visit. But when it's over, I have to admit I feel
more flexible. For writers, mental stretching is even more
important and there are many exercises to help us achieve this.
Creative searches are good because they encourage free
association. However, some writers still need a nudge to go
beyond the obvious. I once set 'potato' as a trigger word in a
writers' workshop. While most students came up with a range of
satellite connections, one student's page was completely filled with
the names of different varieties of potato. That might be fine as a
memory test but it's not much help if you're looking for ideas.

Of course, it happens to the best of us. The brain excels at finding
connections and linking things together. Sometimes, we want it to
do precisely that. Other times, we want it to jump outside the box,
to hop from one category of ideas to another, to look for new
twists and fresh directions. We can encourage it to do this by
disrupting its normal thought patterns. In the following exercise,
you will be asking your brain to do the opposite of what it wants
to do. That isn't easy but it can be liberating when you get the
hang of it. See how you go.

Write a single sentence. Any old sentence will do but here's one to start you off: *It was a dark and stormy night.* You've probably heard that before. It's the famous opener to Edward Bulwer-Lytton's novel *Paul Clifford.* Your task is to follow up with another sentence and then another until your five minutes are over. Now, here comes the tricky bit. Each sentence must have nothing to do with the one preceding it. To resist your brain's natural tendency to establish continuity, try to change your frame of mind in between sentences. Actively break the link and start afresh. Incidentally, this is a fun exercise to do if you belong to a group.

If you find it hard writing whole sentences, do the same thing with single words. For example, take 'balloon' and go from there.

5

Illuminating Objects

What's the connection between home-made raspberry jam, a cocktail shaker, a dog's lead and a baby's bib? According to a well-known kitchen company, they are all answers to the question: 'What object best sums up what happens in your kitchen?' In its marketing literature, the company explains that the chosen items help its designers to understand the customers and what they want from their new kitchen.

It's a clever idea but it's not just for kitchens. In fiction, there's a long tradition of using objects to symbolise aspects of a character or the character's world. Where would Cinderella be without her glass slipper, Mary Poppins without her carpetbag, King Arthur without Excalibur? Similarly, most of us are familiar with Doctor Who's multifunctional sonic screwdriver, Harry Potter's wand, and Sherlock Holmes's violin, which symbolises the dreamy side of the rational detective.

One of the most popular objects for illuminating character is the car. For example, Ian Fleming's choice of an Aston Martin for James Bond reflects 007's status as a top-secret agent, his love of luxury and his phallic power. As Andrew Taylor points out in his article 'Character Driven: Cars in literature',[2] Bond would have struggled to maintain his debonair swagger if he had had to make

---

2 Available on the website drive.com.au

do with a Morris Minor: 'In contrast, the 1960 Jaguar driven by Inspector Morse and Inspector Rebus's old Saab suggest that neither has as many notches on the bedpost as 007.'

But cars are not just for genre fiction. In *The Great Gatsby*, F. Scott Fitzgerald uses them to point up the wealth and extravagance of Jay Gatsby. Gatsby owns several, including a cream-coloured Rolls-Royce – *with a labyrinth of wind-shields that mirrored a dozen suns* – which he uses to ferry his guests to and from the city at weekends.

Sometimes, the meaning of the object is a touch more subtle. In *Brideshead Revisited*, for example, what are we to make of Sebastian Flyte's teddy bear? Is it just an affectation? According to John Mortimer, who adapted the book for television in the 1980s, the bear symbolises Sebastian's failure to grow up. Given that teddy bears are such an intrinsic element of most people's childhoods, Waugh's choice was perfect.

In your own writing, not only can objects help you to convey your characters to readers, but they can also help you develop a character from scratch and even give you ideas for possible plotlines. Try the exercise.

THE EXERCISE

♦ Choose an object that says something about you. When we did this exercise in a writing class, the results were fascinating. One student who'd just had a new baby chose Wet Wipes, someone else chose a watch, and another an onion, which she said signified the many layers of her personality.

♦ Choose three or more objects that represent something meaningful about a new character or one that you've already created. The idea here is that by thinking about the character, imagining the significance of the chosen objects, you will deepen your own understanding of the character's world.

◆ Pick one or two of the following objects and create a brief character sketch based on the object(s).

Car (choose the model)	Map	Iron gate
Patchwork quilt	Wooden box	Restaurant menu
Bunch of keys	Lipstick	Diary
Mirror	Pack of cards	Briefcase

6

Walking in the Rain

While browsing in a National Trust gift shop, a small book entitled *Simple Pleasures* caught my eye. I needed a present for my mother so I had a quick leaf through the pages. I'm not sure what I expected, perhaps something along the lines of 'Make your own ear muffs from grass clippings'. Instead, I found gold: nearly 60 entries by such well-known writers as Sebastian Faulks, Carol Ann Duffy and Alain de Botton.

The premise of the book is that while many of us search for happiness in the big things of life it's the little things that sustain us and keep us going from day to day. The book is a celebration of things that do not require a lottery win to make life pleasurable; things like the sound of owls, the taste of bread and cheese, the feel of rain during an urban run.

What links many of the examples is the natural world, and our primeval connection to it. Our hunter-gatherer ancestors knew nothing of computers or smartphones or any of the gadgets on which our modern world depends. What they had was their five senses and a deep understanding of the landscape around them – the soil, the forest, the rivers and streams.

Of course, it would be a brave – and foolish – soul who wanted to exchange the benefits of 21st-century society for the uncertainty of life as a hunter-gatherer. However, the recent recession and its accompanying austerity have led many in search of a more authentic way of living. Rural crafts like willow-weaving, hedge-laying and basket-making are enjoying a revival. Sewing is popular once more and vintage clothing in charity shops is being snapped up for recycling. And then, there's gardening. Monty Don turned to gardening when his costume jewellery business collapsed during the 1980s economic crisis. 'If you are angry or troubled,' he says, 'nothing provides the same solace as nurturing the soil.'

He's not alone in this opinion. A national charity, THRIVE, aims to create change in the lives of disabled and disadvantaged people through gardening. One of its supporters, the author Sally Brampton, who was once so depressed she tried to commit suicide, explains: 'Gardening keeps you connected into the seasons and keeps you connected into life itself. I think that's really important if you suffer from any kind of mood disorder, to have that kind of optimism, to know that there is always a future.'

A future. That's one of the characteristics of the natural world. Like the old gunslingers in American Westerns, nature never gives up. Even in the urban jungle, rain seeps through cracks in the paving, weeds sprout through the cracks and the sun always rises to nurture new growth.

Of course, not everyone shares this rosy-eyed view. If you're a farmer whose crops have been ruined by months of rain, if your roof has blown off during high winds, if your town has been flooded and you've had to manage without electricity or other basic amenities, you probably think that nature should take a running jump.

For writers, however, what nature offers is an opportunity to engage the reader on a visceral level – the world of physical sensation. Unlike intellectual stimulation, we cannot escape from this. Wherever we live, whoever we are, we all know what it feels like to breathe sweet air, smelly air, air heavy with woodsmoke or damp from rain. We know what it feels to get hiccups, blisters on our feet, or dirt on our hands – and the pleasure of washing it off. Consequently, simple things like shared physical feelings and sensations help to create identification between reader and characters.

But small pleasures do not always come from physical sensation. We are intellectual beings, too. Christina Lamb, whose work as a war correspondent has taken her to some of the world's most dangerous places, once wrote of the pleasure of finding exactly the right change for a Frappuccino in Starbucks. I don't drink Frappuccinos, but I can still identify with the 'right change' motif. Job well done, I think, every time I manage to empty my purse of all those small coins.

Then there are the quirky things, like being the first person to notice that a fresh checkout has just opened in the supermarket, finding something you thought you had lost, or – and I accept that this might be a very personal one – descaling the kettle. For writer and journalist Valerie Grove, it's picking up litter while walking her dog: 'But I'm not doing it *pro bono publico*: I'm doing it selfishly, for me. Anyway, it's really enjoyable. I win friends and may even influence people. Why not try it and see?'

However lofty our dreams and ambitions, our lives are grounded in the everyday and that's worth exploring. Try the following exercise.

THE EXERCISE

Compile a list of your own small pleasures, the things that lift your spirits and keep you going. At the end of every day, add another to your list.

A variation is to compile a list of pleasures from specific times in your life. A childhood list, for example, might help to awaken some long-forgotten memories, some of which you could explore in a longer piece.

$$\overset{\displaystyle 7}{\bigcirc}$$

Buckets of Inspiration

Every so often a film comes along that captures the public imagination, and changes lives. One such film is *The Bucket List,* starring Jack Nicholson as Edward, and Morgan Freeman as Carter, two terminally ill men who share a hospital room. Edward is a corporate tycoon, whose company owns the hospital. Carter is a garage mechanic. 'You might want to do something about the pea soup,' says Carter, whose hopes of studying to become a history professor were dashed by his need to earn money to support a family.

What unites the two is their decision to make a list of all the things they'd like to do before they 'kick the bucket'. There's the usual ambitious stuff – skydiving, climbing the pyramids, riding motorbikes over the Great Wall of China – but other wishes are more thoughtful. Carter wants to 'laugh until I cry'; Edward (with a little pushing from Carter) wants to 'help a complete stranger for the good'.

The big exploits add spectacle but the main focus of the film is the developing friendship between the two men and the psychological healing that results from their shared journey. In the end, the central theme – that whatever your situation, it's never too late to be proactive – is the one that resonates. Stripped to the bone, it's the same premise that underpins all successful stories. Actions have consequences – and sometimes even the smallest action can radically change our life's path.

The film touched a chord. Soon, bucket lists popped up on the social networking sites and the term made it into the online Urban Dictionary. Enter 'bucket list' into your Internet search engine and you'll be spoilt for choice. There are specialised bucket list ideas: for winter, for teenagers, for travel, and so on. I even found a 'Dark Sky' bucket list for fans of astronomy – and Professor Brian Cox.

Clearly, it isn't necessary to be ill to make use of the bucket list concept. When librarian Lesley Evans found herself dreading her 60th birthday she decided to compile a wish list of 60 things she'd never done and work her way through them during the following year. What made her list different was its modest goals. There is no skydiving, no trips around the world, no sex in aircraft loos. Instead, Mrs Evans wanted to visit the British Library, drink sambuca, and attend a Women's Institute meeting. As she explained when the media picked up her story, the goals had to be achievable: 'I think experience makes you a more interesting person and this is something that anyone of any age can do. They were all things I had particularly wanted to do but had just never got around to.'

Although the intention of a bucket list is to motivate a person to set goals, the items chosen can also reveal much about the character of that person, which is good news for writers. Psychologist Christopher Peterson, whose research focuses on positive psychology (the science of what makes life worth living), points out that many bucket lists contain 'narcissistic' items such as 'getting a tattoo'. Others, by contrast, are more focused on things that connect the writer to 'something larger than themselves, typically other people and their welfare'. Someone who wants to take their entire family on a cruise would fit into the latter category, but it could be volunteering, making time for an elderly relative or, like Edward in *The Bucket List,* helping a complete stranger for the good.

As writers, we can use the bucket list concept in many different ways. The following exercises will give you ideas.

THE EXERCISES

◆ If you're new to the concept of bucket lists, start by spending five minutes compiling one of your own. If you want to follow Lesley Evans' example of listing achievable goals for the next year, that's fine. If you'd like to climb Everest or go whitewater rafting, that's OK, too. However, try to include a variety of items, rather than getting stuck in a category rut. Mention people you'd like to see, places to go, skills to learn, activities to try, and so on. Be as quirky as you like. If you want to build a sandcastle or have a colonic irrigation, go ahead. It's your list.

◆ Once you've created a bucket list for yourself, try doing one from the point of view of a character. If you already have a character in mind, use the list to explore the character more deeply. Alternatively, you can use it to create a brand-new character. For every item, ask yourself: what does this reveal about my character? Is there a pattern to the list? I recently read a list in which almost every item involved watching something – going to an air display, visiting an art gallery, watching sport, and so on. I asked the writer if he regarded himself as one of life's spectators and he agreed that he was. If you belong to a writers' circle, ask your fellow members what they deduce about the character from the items you've included. What age is the character? What gender? Are they introvert or extravert? Imaginative or practical?

◆ Another option is to compile a sensory bucket list. What do you like to see, hear, smell, taste and touch? In real life, our dominant sense is vision and consequently when we sit down to write we may forget to use the other four. Touch is the most neglected but its inclusion enhances a reader's experience on a visceral level, thereby making your scene both real and memorable. I still remember the slight shiver I felt when one of Jilly Cooper's characters walked barefoot on wet grass.

8

The Writing on the Wall

'If walls could talk,' goes the old saying. But of course they can. Anyone who's had to strip umpteen layers of wallpaper before redecorating will know what I mean. Each ghastly layer clings to its predecessor like chewing gum on a shoe, until finally you find THE WALL. And guess what, it's orange. What on earth...? And then you remember that you once painted your bedroom wall purple. Well, maybe you didn't. You were probably more sensible. But I did. What's worse, I painted the opposite wall in 'crushed apricot'. Well, that was student life in the Sixties.

But there's more to walls than the annoyance of replacing someone else's decorating disasters. Walls are historical artefacts and when you start stripping, you never know what you'll find. It might be a frieze or a moulding, smothered by anaglypta. It could be a serving hatch hidden behind a thin piece of ply. Or it could be something that poses a puzzle. When new owners started renovating the Glenisle Hotel in Scotland, they found sealed-up doorways behind the wallpaper. Two of the doorways were on the first floor and led to the outside. As they said: 'We know that there have never been other rooms or other buildings there so we cannot imagine where these doors used to go.'

Writers can have fun with this kind of detail. Possibilities abound, ranging from the sinister to the quirky. In *A Not so Perfect Crime* by Catalan author Teresa Solana (translated by Peter Bush) two incompetent private detectives, Eduard and Borja, can't afford a swanky office but still want to impress their clients. So they resort to fakery. To give the impression they have a secretary, they dress an empty reception desk with a little bottle of red Chanel nail varnish, a Liberty foulard, and a copy of *Hello!* And then:

> *With characteristic cunning, Borja has had very flash imitation-mahogany doors set in one of the walls (the carpenter has yet to be paid, I fear) mounted with a couple of gilt plaques that proclaim our names and respective posts in italics.*

Behind these fake doors, the non-existent offices are always being painted or redecorated. It's a neat touch.

Of course, you don't need fake doors to create an illusion. Murals and *trompe l'oeil* have been around for centuries and are still popular. Alexander McPherson, an artist with a background in theatre set design, has created 'Fantasy Flight' murals for children's hospital wards, a 'Tuscan Garden' in a dining room, and a large mural based on Enid Blyton's *The Faraway Tree*, which covers all four walls of a child's bedroom. For instant effect, *trompe l'oeil* wallpaper and fabric hangings are readily available. You can have the steps of Montmartre leading out of your bathroom, a railway line in your kitchen, and the corridor of a castle in your downstairs loo.

In real life, *trompe l'oeil* gives blank walls a narrative. In fiction, the concept of *trompe l'oeil* enables walls to take on the archetypal shapeshifter role. In the Harry Potter stories, for example, what looks like a brick wall on platform $9^3/_4$ is actually a portal into the world of Hogwarts. In the film *Being John Malkovitch,* the main character discovers a portal in the wall behind an office filing cabinet. He crawls through and finds himself in the head of John Malkovitch, the actor, who is in the process of ordering towels from an online retailer. For 15 minutes he can see, hear and feel everything that JM is experiencing. He and a colleague start selling the John Malkovich experience for $200 a pop. It sounds silly, I know, but the film poses questions about reality, identity and how we construct them.

The Yellow Wallpaper by Charlotte Perkins Gilman is rather more disturbing. First published in 1892, it centres on a young woman who moves to the country with her husband to recover from post-natal depression. She likes to write but 19th-century paternalism forbids intellectual stimulation. With nothing to do, she becomes obsessed by the wallpaper in her bedroom:

It is stripped off – the paper in great patches all around the head of my bed, about as far as I can reach, and in a great place on the other side of the room low down. I never saw a worse paper in my life. One of those sprawling flamboyant patterns committing every artistic sin ... The colour is repellent, almost revolting; a smouldering unclean yellow, strangely faded by the slow-turning sunlight.

As the character's paranoia grows, she imagines women are trapped behind the wallpaper, including her. She starts to strip off the paper. The story ends with her descent into madness: *'I've got out at last,' said I ... 'And I've pulled off most of the paper, so you can't put me back!'*

The Yellow Wallpaper has been adapted numerous times for stage, radio and screen, most recently in 2011 for a film starring Aric Cushing. Like most successful fiction, its themes and motifs can inspire new stories, whose content may be very different from that of the original. I even found echoes in a story by Steven Moffat in the 2006 *Doctor Who Annual.* In 'What I did in my Summer Holidays – by Sally Sparrow', a young girl goes to stay with her aunt and starts to pick at the peeling yellow wallpaper in the guest bedroom. You won't be surprised to learn that time travel is involved. It's a good read. Find it on the BBC website: www.bbc.co.uk/doctorwho/s4/features/stories/ fiction_blink_the_original_story_01

You, too, can be inspired. Try the following exercise.

THE EXERCISE

Write for five minutes, using one of these triggers:

- You have just moved to a house/flat in need of redecoration. As you take your scraper to the old wallpaper, you uncover some writing on the plaster. It is a message addressed to you. It could be a warning, a threat, a cry for help, or even a riddle. You decide.

- You have just moved to a brand-new house/flat. Before you put up your own wallcovering, you write something on the blank wall for posterity. It could be a drawing. Or even a prediction. I heard of a decorator who stripped back a wall to find 'MANCHESTER CITY WILL WIN THE PREMIERSHIP IN 2009' spray-painted on the plaster. (Oops – the winner was Manchester United.)

- You have just moved to a house/flat in which one wall has been covered with realistic bibliotheque *trompe l'oeil* paper. You prefer real books so you plan to remove the paper. However, there's something strange about this paper. The books keep rearranging themselves. What is going on?

- While stripping back kitchen tiles, you find a hidden door. It doesn't lead to another room in your house, nor does it lead to the outside. Could it be a portal? If so, to where? Explore.

9

Fabulous Failure

Fabulous isn't a word you'd normally associate with failure but it's certainly worked out that way for Stephen Pile, who once founded a club called *The Not Terribly Good Club of Great Britain*. After receiving thousands of applications for membership, the club eventually closed, having been deemed too successful to continue. Pile's official handbook of the club, *The Book of Heroic Failures*, first published in 1978, became a bestseller and went through numerous reprints.

In 2011, Pile did it again with *The Ultimate Book of Heroic Failures,* an all-new collection of blunders, bungling and sheer bad luck. Like the explorer who was invited to give a lecture on survival techniques to a school in Devon. While out for a stroll, he fell over a cliff. It took 40 local people, two helicopters and a tracker dog five hours to find him.

What makes failure so appealing? Writing in *The Sunday Times,* Stephen Pile suggests it's to do with our approach to happiness, which lies in 'not only accepting that things go belly up but also rejoicing in them when they do'. He cites John Sergeant, the political commentator whose accident-waiting-to-happen performances on *Strictly Come Dancing* endeared him to the public.

I would argue that there's something even more basic at work. While we may aim for excellence ourselves and we admire

excellence in others, the person who never makes a mistake is just
– well, boring. Failure is a fundamental part of being human, so
when we see others making a hash of things – provided it's not
while they're fixing our hair or teeth – we know the person has
something in common with us and we warm to them.

Comedy scriptwriters have always capitalised on this when
creating characters. Way back, there was Charlie Chaplin's
accident-prone tramp. On television, classic series like *Fawlty
Towers*, *The Office* and, more recently, *Miranda*, all feature main
characters with a talent for messing up.

In fiction, failure is also useful for creating tension. By casting
doubt on a character's ability to get out of trouble or reach a
goal, the story is less predictable. We bite our nails, wondering if
and how the character will succeed. This also adds depth to the
character. If you're a *Doctor Who* fan, for example, you may have
noticed how the newer doctors are more fallible than the earlier
incarnations. They come through in the end, but their assistants
often play a crucial role in their success. In one of the best David
Tennant episodes, for example, *The Family of Blood,* the Doctor
believes he is a human schoolteacher with no special powers. He
falls in love but has no idea how to be romantic. He falls down
stairs. When his life is threatened, he is vulnerable and scared. It's
up to Martha Jones, his assistant, to bring him to his senses and
save his life.

A third useful attribute of failure in fiction is its ability to make
unsympathetic characters likeable. Ed Reardon, the creation of
Christopher Douglas and Andrew Nickolds in *Ed Reardon's Week*,
is one of the most pompous characters ever to make it into a
seventh series on Radio 4. If he were successful he would be

insufferable. But he isn't successful. He's a has-been writer and constantly on the brink of running out of money. Having lost his house in a divorce settlement, he now lives in a small flat with his cat, and spends his days railing against the modern world. Almost nothing goes right for him. In the following extract from the book of *Ed Reardon's Week,* he attempts to get change for the photocopier in his local library:

> *'Can I just direct your attention to the notice at this time,' said the functionary who must have begun the lengthy librarian's qualification process shortly after his seventh birthday.*

> *'Yes, I know it says "No Change Given" but you see I've only got a two pound coin, and the photocopier doesn't give change either.'*

> *'Well, if you were to purchase a beverage or muffin from Café Da Vinci – we have Blueberry or Famous Regular at this time.'*

> *'I don't want a muffin. I want a 20p,' I shouted, banging my fist on the issue desk.*

> *'I'm afraid we're not allowed to give change, Sir. Now is there anything else I can help you with at this time?'*

There can't be many of us who haven't come up against this kind of brick-wall intransigence, so we know exactly how it feels. As a result, we sympathise with Ed. His daily irritations are our daily irritations.

So there you have it, three great reasons for not rejecting failure. Use it to create believable characters who are more interesting to the reader, to rack up tension by making your character's fate less predictable, and to engender liking for unsympathetic characters.

THE EXERCISE

Remember the old dictum to write what you know? Fortunately, when it comes to making a mess of things, most of us have more material than we can handle. Why not make use of it? Compile your own list of bungles, fiascos and occasions on which things didn't quite work out as you'd planned. Nothing is too small to mention. Jilly Cooper first came to fame with an article in which she catalogued her domestic disasters, including the time she failed to notice a red silk handkerchief in the whites wash. As a result, her husband Leo was the only man in the rugger team with a rose-pink jockstrap. The incident didn't go to waste. She used it in her fiction. We can all learn from her example.

Once you have your list, keep adding to it. Then you'll never be short of a fabulous failure.

Comic Wordplay

When I taught writing classes on a Monday evening, I always listened to *I'm Sorry I Haven't a Clue* on Radio 4 while driving to the venue. If you've ever tuned in to this, you'll know that it describes itself as 'the antidote to panel games' and involves lots of comic wordplay. My favourite was, and still is, the round in which panellists have to think of new definitions for existing words. For example: Reincarnation – to be born again as a tin of condensed milk; Awol – a dyslexic owl; Offset – the regulating authority that inspects badgers.

Many of the definitions have to be spoken aloud before they 'click' and many are a bit risqué, but the programme's brilliant ability to push the boundaries of the English language ensured that I always arrived at my class in a good mood. This particular segment of the show proved so popular that it generated its own *Uxbridge English Dictionary,* which one reviewer described as 'The funniest book I have EVER read'.

Sometimes, if we had a spare five minutes during that Monday class, I would suggest that my students try coining some definitions of their own. One man, a retired geography teacher, was always able to come up with a string of very funny items, although it's fair to say that most students found it challenging. But that is good. As writers, we need to challenge our creative brain in as many ways as we can. To be creative is to have the ability to think outside the box, to see things from different angles, to reach ideas that are not immediately obvious to other people.

Fortunately, there are thought processes we can cultivate to help us with this. Psychologists who have studied the creative process often point out that there are no truly new ideas. Rather, new ideas are generated from combining existing ideas or in rearranging old elements to make new associations. Previously remote, or unconnected, elements of thought suddenly become linked in a way that strikes people, including readers, as fresh. If we apply this process to the word 'palisade' for example, we start by splitting the existing two syllables apart. This leaves us with 'palis' and 'ade'. Now, 'palis' sounds the same as 'palace' and 'ade' sounds like the last syllable of a fizzy drink. So, we now have a new association between the two syllables. Slap them together again and you have palace-ade – the new definition of which, according to the *Uxbridge English Dictionary,* is what the Queen drinks.

There are plenty of words in the English language that end in 'ade' and you can use the same strategy with those, too. For example, what would you make of 'stockade'? According to the UED, it's fizzy Oxo. How about 'lemonade'? That's already a drink so we need to lose the liquid association and think of another. 'Ade' sounds the same as 'aid' so maybe lemonade could be a charity for impoverished citrus fruit. You get the idea?

Of course, not every word is amenable to a new definition but once you start looking at individual syllables you'll be surprised what jumps out at you. Then, it's just a question of playing around with the components until you hit something that works. It takes practice but it's a great creative workout. Try the following exercise.

The following words invite redefinition. Have a go. Hint: say the word aloud, and try changing where the stress falls.

catatonic	antithesis	brandish
tentacle	mistake	coolant
counterintuitive	phobia	gullet

Alternatively, open your dictionary, find some suitable words and make up some new definitions. Hint: once you have a useful suffix, like –ant, for example, you can use Google to find other words that end with that suffix. Then you're on a roll.

Putting on the Style

'I'm a literary writer,' someone said to me recently, 'but no one wants to buy my work.' When he showed me some of this work, I wasn't surprised. His style was so tortuous, so self-consciously elaborate that it read more like a parody of literature than a genuine attempt to communicate with the reader. And beneath the style, there was no supporting narrative. He then went on to tell me – a touch dismissively – that he'd had quite a few stories published in mass-market magazines. I read one of these and found it well crafted, well plotted and perfect for its market. So what, I wanted to know, was the problem?

'Oh, those,' he said with a shrug, 'they're just trash. I'm a literary writer.'

After a bit of probing I realised that what he really wanted was to describe the human condition without its usual framework of structure, plot and characterisation. He believed – and he's not alone in this belief – that literary style transcends the nuts and bolts of story.

But style and story are two different things. Story is what you have to say, style is how you say it. And, as Strunk and White point out in *The Elements of Style*, style is not 'a sauce by which a dull dish is made palatable'. That said, style is an intrinsic component of writing – and indeed speaking – that significantly affects the flavour of the content. For example, a meteorologist forecasting the weather will use official weatherspeak like 'bright intervals' and 'scattered showers'. Someone talking to their next-door neighbour will use everyday conversation style. 'What a lovely day,' they'll say, or 'It's a bit chilly.'

For new writers of fiction, developing a distinctive style can be a bit of a headache. The usual advice is not to worry too much and simply wait for 'your' style to develop naturally. 'As you become proficient in the use of language, your style will emerge,' write Strunk and White, 'because you yourself will emerge . . .'

While this is true, it suggests that style is something that just happens, when in fact we all – both writers and non-writers – effortlessly adjust our language depending on context. Poets don't speak poetically when buying train tickets or complaining to the local council that their bin hasn't been emptied. Politicians don't use fancy rhetoric when speaking to their families. And many writers consciously use different styles for different kinds of writing. The James Bond novel *Devil May Care*, for example, was written not by Ian Fleming but by Sebastian Faulks, who described the style as 80 per cent Fleming. 'My Bond,' he said, 'is Fleming's Bond.'

Many brilliant writers learn their craft by experimenting with different styles. Joan Didion, for example, cites Henry James and Ernest Hemingway as major influences. But while James's sentences were complicated, and made her afraid to put words down, Hemingway's were perfect and very direct: 'Those sentences just knocked me out. In fact, I taught myself to type by typing out the beginning of *Farewell to Arms* and a couple of short stories. I was just trying to learn how to type, but you get those rhythms in your head.'

Similarly, when Raymond Chandler wanted to become a writer, he took an Erle Stanley Gardner crime story to pieces and rewrote it, sentence by sentence, to find out how it was done. That didn't make him into a paler version of Gardner. He went on to become a brilliant wordsmith with his own distinctive style.

So, let's not be too precious about style. If you think of it as a path, rather than a destination, you never know where it will lead. Along the way, take a look at Raymond Queneau's fabulously quirky *Exercises in Style*. A French intellectual, mathematician and poet, Queneau was fascinated by language and what it could achieve. His starting point for the book is a 'pointless' incident, the kind of thing that could happen to anyone:

> *On a crowded Paris bus at midday, the narrator observes a young man accusing another of jostling him deliberately. When a vacant seat appears, the young man rushes to occupy it. Later, in another part of town, the narrator spots the man again, being advised by a friend to sew another button on his overcoat.*

Queneau takes this anecdote and retells it in 99 different styles, including a publisher's blurb for a novel, an official letter, and an opera. He uses different voices, too, different grammatical and rhetorical forms, different genres, and even slang. Each is a brilliant snapshot of how a writer's choices can radically affect both the tone of a piece and the reader's perception of the main character. Here, for example, is the first sentence of a piece called *Feminine*, which today we might call chick-lit:

> *Lot of clots! Today round about midday (goodness it was hot, just as well I'd put Odorono under my arms otherwise my*

little cretonne summer dress that my little dressmaker who
makes things specially cheaply for me made for me would
have had it) near the Parc Monceau (it's nicer than the
Luxembourg where I send my son, the idea of getting alopecia
at his age) the bus came, it was full, but I made eyes at the
conductor and got in.

OK, so it's exaggerated, but then so are all the pieces. Queneau
pushed style to its limits, not to make fun of it, as some have
suggested, but rather to act as a linguistic 'rust remover', allowing
the possibilities of language to be shown in stark relief. Although
first published in 1947, the book continues to inspire modern
writers, including Philip Pullman, who described it as 'endlessly
fascinating and very funny' and Matt Madden, whose *99 Ways to*
Tell a Story is a comic-strip version.

Experimenting with style in short pieces is a great route to
becoming more confident about your writing. The beauty of
Queneau's approach is that it imposes no narrative constraints
and this allows you to concentrate on the 'how' rather than the
'what'.

THE EXERCISES

Choose one of the following options.

◆ If you are a beginner, try following Joan Didion's example of copying a short piece
of prose from a favourite author. When you've finished, read the next one or two
(uncopied) sentences, put the original aside, and write the sentences from memory.
Do yours differ from the originals? If so, how? Do this regularly and you will find,
as Didion found, the 'rhythms in your head'.

◆ Try rewriting this sentence by Shakespeare in less poetic style: *All the world's a*
stage and all the men and women merely players. Compose a few variations and see

what happens. If Shakespeare is too daunting, try this line from Thomas Paine: *What we obtain too cheap, we esteem too lightly.*

◆ Take an ordinary event, such as a person catching a train, buying a paper or visiting a coffee shop. The person drops something by mistake and a stranger picks it up and hands it back. The stranger smiles and tries to start a conversation. Now, do a 'Queneau'. Rewrite the incident in five (or 99 if you like!) completely different ways. For example, you could write one piece as a chatty letter, another as stream of consciousness, another in flashback and so on. Try purple prose with long sentences and lots of adjectives, followed by short sentences and no adjectives. It's up to you.

12

Finding the Key

I recently unpacked some of my belongings that have been in storage for two years. A lot of things went straight in the bin. Others were like old friends I'd almost forgotten. Then, among a pile of papers, I came across a key; a long, thin key on a decorative key ring. I have no idea what this key is for or why I kept it. Should I throw it out? Or hang on to it, just in case?

That's the thing about keys. We can't tell what they'll open just by looking at them. And when we find a locked door, we cannot know for sure what key will fit it. In fiction, the key is an archetypal device for locking and unlocking, not just doors, but the story itself. Rich in symbolism, the key can be both literal and metaphorical. Take a look at this extract from *Alice in Wonderland* by Lewis Carroll:

> *There were doors all round the hall, but they were all locked; and when Alice had been all the way down one side and up the other, trying every door, she walked sadly down the middle, wondering how she was ever to get out again. Suddenly she came upon a little three-legged table, all made of solid glass; there was nothing on it except a tiny golden key, and Alice's first thought was that it might belong to one of the doors of the hall; but, alas! either the locks were too large, or the key was too small, but at any rate it would not open any of them. However, on the second time round, she came upon a low curtain she had not noticed before, and behind it was a little*

*door about fifteen inches high: she tried the little golden key
in the lock, and to her great delight it fitted!*

Alice's discovery of the key and – more important – her decision
to use it corresponds to what mythologist Joseph Campbell called
'The Crossing of the First Threshold', beyond which lies the
unknown. In real life, we often baulk at such thresholds.
According to Campbell: *The usual person is more than content, he
is even proud, to remain within the indicated bounds, and popular
belief gives him every reason to fear so much as the first step into
the unknown.* In fiction, however, main characters must cross the
threshold, assume the role of 'the hero' and start their journey –
otherwise there'd be no story.

In *Alice,* the literal key is also symbolic, in that it links Alice's
world of sheltered Victorian childhood with a new, more
challenging one in which she takes charge. Similarly, in Frances
Hodgson Burnett's *The Secret Garden,* Mary Lennox's journey to
physical and spiritual healing begins when she finds the key to a
neglected walled garden in the grounds of her uncle's mansion on
the moor. The garden has been locked since her aunt's death.
Like Alice, Mary makes the decision to use the key. She and two
friends restore the garden. As new life sprouts from the soil, the
children, too, are transformed. It's a wonderfully uplifting story.

In both *Alice* and *The Secret Garden,* a key provides access,
allowing the characters to move from a disempowered space to
one of autonomy and enlightenment. However, as anyone who's
ever bought a magnifying mirror will know, enlightenment is not
always a pleasant experience. In Perrault's folk tale *Bluebeard,*
Bluebeard's new bride unlocks a room he has forbidden her to
enter. She finds the floor swimming in blood and her husband's

previous wives hanging on hooks. Here, the key opens not just a door but also her mind to Bluebeard's brutal nature.

But keys are not just for folk tales and children's fiction. Dan Brown delights in using keys, both real and symbolic. In *The Da Vinci Code*, for example, the gold fleur-de-lis key belonging to Jacques Saunière symbolises his status as grand master of the Priory of Sion, the society whose secrets are so sacred he is willing to die to protect them. But this key also unlocks a Swiss bank deposit box. When his granddaughter, Sophie, and Robert Langdon use the key to access the box, they find a 'cryptex', a locked cylinder, which Langdon identifies as a *clef de voûte* – the literal meaning of which is the key to the vault. However, as Langdon explains to Sophie, *clef de voûte* is also an architectural term that refers to archways or ceilings. Sophie is confused:

'But vaulted ceilings don't have keys.'

'Actually, they do. Every stone archway requires a central wedge-shaped stone at the top which locks the pieces together and carries all the weight. This stone is, in architectural terms, the key to the vault. In English, we call it a keystone.'

Langdon suspects that they have found the Priory keystone, a Masonic artefact that is itself an encoded map revealing the hiding place of the Holy Grail. In *The Da Vinci Code,* almost everything provides a 'key' to something else, whether it be a real key, a cryptex or a riddle the characters must decode before they can proceed. It's *Alice in Wonderland* again, but set in more glamorous locations and with car chases.

If you like the idea of using keys in your fiction, it's well worth exploring their many meanings in the real world. For example, keys are symbols of power, status and privilege. In the corporate arena, high-flying employees are often rewarded with a key to the executive loo. In some countries, distinguished visitors might receive a 'Key to the City', symbolising the city's willingness to let them come and go freely. And, as every romantic knows, keys are popular in jewellery. The poet Frederick Saunders once wrote of lovers giving their hearts to each other, locking them up and throwing away the key – but probably not if the key came from the upmarket jeweller Tiffany, where a fleur-de-lis key pendant with diamonds will set you back nearly £6,000.

Try the following exercise.

THE EXERCISE

Either do a creative search with 'key' as your trigger, or choose just one of the following ideas as inspiration:

◆ You discover a key in an old cupboard. You quickly realise that this is a skeleton key. It will open any door. What will you do with this key?

◆ Keys are revealing in terms of character – as is the key ring. Key rings come in all sizes and shapes, including Formula One racing cars, personalised handprints, and even takeaway food tags. What sort of person has a key ring engraved with 'I love pizza'? Create a fictional bunch of keys. What does each key – and the ring – tell you about the person who owns it?

◆ If you could have the key (real or symbolic) to just one door, where would it lead?

◆ In Grimm's fairytale *The Golden Key,* a boy finds a key and a small locked box buried under snow in the forest. The story ends without revealing what wonderful things are in the box. Use your own imagination to finish the story. (*The Golden Key* is very short. If you want to read it, find it online.)

Note: Creative search is the technique of writing a trigger word or topic in the centre of a blank page and using it to generate a galaxy of associations. As each new thought comes to you, jot it down as a word or short phrase, circle it, and draw lines between circles that are connected or related. Keep going until you have a large web of satellite ideas. My students often refer to this as a spidergram or mind web. Tony Buzan invented his own version and called it a Mind Map. Though the methods vary in their specifics, the same basic principle underpins them all. If we brainstorm ideas in a non-linear fashion, grouping similar concepts together without being constrained by them, we open our minds to a potentially unlimited source of inspiration. You can find more information, including some fancy diagrams and lots more resources, on the Internet.

13

You Know Something About . . .

In *A Moveable Feast*, Ernest Hemingway talks about his life as a struggling, and often hungry, writer, living in Paris in the 1920s. Sometimes the work went well, but on other days – usually when he was starting a new story – inspiration deserted him. On those days, Hemingway would sit in front of the fire in his work room, squeeze orange peel into the flame and watch it sputter. He would then get up and stand looking out over the city skyline before trying to reassure himself.

I don't know about you but I find it heartening to think that a writer of Hemingway's calibre might be stuck for words. Fortunately for posterity, Hemingway had a trick for getting himself out of this rut. All he had to do, he kept telling himself, was to write 'one true sentence' and take it from there:

> *It was easy then because there was always one true sentence that I knew or had seen or had heard someone say . . . Up in that room I decided that I would write one story about each thing that I knew about. I was trying to do this all the time I was writing, and it was good and severe discipline.*

One true sentence on something he knew about. It's a very simple idea, but don't be fooled. It is also powerful. And if it worked for Hemingway, it might also work for you. Remember, though, that we're not talking here about things you know how to *do*, like driving a car, cooking pasta, or building a web page. Rather, we're talking about personal experience. For example, you know what happened in your life today, what thoughts you had, what people you saw, and so on. Simple things like these are often all you need to begin a story.

Similarly, you know what it feels like to stub your toe, to get grit in your eye, to drink a glass of iced water when you're feeling hot. If you live in a town, you know what it feels like to walk down the street and smell onions, pizza and coffee wafting out of the fast-food joints. If you live in the country, you're probably more familiar with cows, wood smoke, and maybe hawthorn on a late spring evening.

Sometimes what we know best is an emotional state. We all know what frightens us, what thrills us, what makes us happy or sad. Film director Steven Spielberg has often spoken about the childhood insecurities that drive his work. Picked on at school, he was lonely and fearful, particularly of the dark: 'I had no way to sublimate or channel those fears until I began telling stories to my younger sisters. This removed the fear from my soul and transferred it right into theirs.' He's been doing the same thing ever since, to the delight of audiences all over the world.

If none of the above works for you, you know what you're doing right now – even if it's only staring at the wall. That, too, can be fruitful. The *Paris Review* once asked E. L. Doctorow what came first in his writing – character or theme. The multi-award-winning Doctorow admitted that sometimes it was a moment of personal desperation:

*For instance, with Ragtime, I was so desperate to write
something, I was facing the wall of my study in my house in
New Rochelle and so I started to write about the wall... Then
I wrote about the house that was attached to the wall. It was
built in 1906, you see, so I thought about the era and what
Broadview Avenue looked like then: trolley cars ran along the
avenue down at the bottom of the hill; people wore white
clothes in the summer to stay cool . . . One thing led to
another and that's the way that book began.*

The rest, as they say, is history. The book *Ragtime* became a film
and then a hit musical. At the time of writing, it is running at
Regent's Park Open Air Theatre in London. Like Hemingway,
Doctorow learned to 'trust the act of writing' to show him the
way.

I can't promise that you'll be as successful in your writing as
Hemingway, Spielberg or Doctorow, but I can promise you that
every time you sit down to write, you know enough to get yourself
started. And just in case you are wondering, here's the first
sentence of *Ragtime*: *In 1902, father built a house at the crest of
the Broadway Avenue hill in New Rochelle, New York.*

Try the following exercise.

THE EXERCISE

'I know something about love,' sang Vonda Shepard in the song of the same
name. What do you know something about? Make a list.

As an alternative, make a list starting with 'I don't know about...'

When you have your list, choose one item to explore in more detail.

14

Go Exploring

According to Alvaro Fernandez, the co-founder of the market research company SharpBrains, a simple way to exercise your brain is to explore new locations. As he says in an article entitled 'The Ten Habits of Highly Effective Brains',[3] 'Adapting to new locations forces you to pay more attention to your environment.'

This is true. The brain is hard-wired to pay more attention to new things, so the more new things you can offer it, the better you exercise it. We all know how energising it can be to visit a foreign country or even an unfamiliar place in our own country. For example, I love going to London because there are so many different things to see – shops, art galleries, museums – all with their own smells, sounds and atmosphere. But I also love Paris, with which I'm not so familiar. As a result, I notice quirky things, like the way the chairs outside cafes all face the street, as though the pavement were a stage. When I mentioned this to a French friend, she laughed. To her, it's just the way it's always been.

For writers, of course, the idea is to train yourself to see even familiar environments with a fresh eye. When Alexander McCall Smith chose Suffolk as the location for his wartime novel *La's Orchestra Saves the World,* he already knew the county from his childhood. But as he explained in a radio interview, he needed to

---

3   Available on the website sharpbrains.com

reacquaint himself in order to add texture to his characters' surroundings. He went back to tour the villages: 'I was soaking up the atmosphere,' he said. 'I love those little lanes that you've got in Suffolk with the old metal road signs still there...I was also looking for the vegetation, what was growing at the edge of the road, things like that and looking at people's gardens. I'm familiar with some of the lovely houses and one of the things I love about the county is the faint pink wash.'

It's that attention to small things like narrow lanes, roadside plants, the colour of buildings, that gives readers a real sense of 'being there'. But it's not just the way a place looks that gives it character. For Dorinne Kondo, an anthropologist who went to Tokyo to study Japanese culture, it's often a sound that triggers her memory. See how she brings the city to life in this extract from *Crafting Selves*:

> *Turning the corner on the way to my apartment, I would always hear the clanking of the metal presses in the distance, as they stamp out parts for heavy machinery or cut out food containers, belt buckles, even Snoopy medallions from sheets of plastic. Most of these puresuyasan, as they are called, are one- or two-person operations, where the machines beat out their insistent rhythms in the room adjoining the main house. Our days were punctuated by the relentless pulsing of the presses. If you were to venture beyond the bounds of the neighbourhood and take a walk to the station, other sounds would provide accompaniment. The whine of machines at the neighbourhood shoe factory deafens passersby, and a penetrating aroma – glue for the soles, I was told – emanates from the open windows and doors.*

Note how that vividness comes not from visual detail, but from Kondo's use of specific sounds to conjure up the atmosphere of this particular Tokyo neighbourhood. By listening to those sounds, we, too, can experience the feeling of walking down the roads and streets. The smell of glue adds to our experience. Similarly, if your story was set in the country, you'd want to put in details that would give the reader a sense of being there. Your reader may never have smelled wild garlic, seen rosebay willowherb or trodden in cow dung, but such details will still give the piece that important illusion of reality.

THE EXERCISE

Next time you find yourself in an unfamiliar environment, take out your notebook and jot down as many details about the place as you can. Ask yourself questions. If there are buildings, of what are they constructed: Stone? Brick? Wood? If there are trees or flowers, do you recognise them? Look for leaf shapes, colours, textures.

Is the air fresh? Or not? Most places are a mixture of different smells. Take a deep breath and see if you can identify the various ingredients – or perhaps one that overwhelms all the others. When I lived in Dublin, the smell of roasting barley from the Guinness brewery wafted over the River Liffey near O'Connell Bridge. That's a highly specific scent that characterised Dublin life.

What sounds can you hear? Close your eyes and listen. Finally, a tip from photographer and broadcaster Lucinda Lambton, whose daily mantra is 'To look up is to learn to love architecture: 'Look around and about you, and best of all above you, and, more often than not, you will see something that will straightway suffuse you with satisfaction.'

Lambton's tip works even when there's no architecture and nothing above except empty sky. Release your inner child and lie on your back, as Laurie Lee does in *Cider with Rosie*:

Chewing grass on our backs, the grass scaffolding the sky, the summer was all we heard; cuckoos crossed distances on chains of cries, flies buzzed and choked in the ears, and the saw-toothed chatter of mowing machines drifted on waves of air from the fields.

$$\left(\!\!\begin{array}{c}15\end{array}\!\!\right)$$

Six-Word Stories

Ernest Hemingway once supposedly bet his friends that he could write a complete story in six words. His friends accepted the bet and Hemingway wrote his story on a napkin: *For sale: baby shoes. Never worn.*

This is masterful stuff, a perfect example of what has become known as Hemingway's 'iceberg' principle, in which the words on the page are just the visible tip of the story. Rather, it is the invisible – or missing – content that allows the images to blossom into meaning.

But did Hemingway actually write that story? Or is it an urban legend? No one seems to know. The concept, however, has proved inspirational. In 2006, the magazine *Wired* asked dozens of its favourite sci-fi, fantasy, and horror writers for their take on the topic. In the same year, online magazine *Smith* added a personal twist when it used Hemingway's story to inspire readers to contribute their life story in just six words. Contributions flooded in and the best were published in a book, *Not Quite What I Was Planning: And Other Six-Word Memoirs by Writers Famous and Obscure*. More books followed.

Other online journals and networking sites have jumped on the bandwagon. Just enter 'six-word stories Hemingway' into your search engine and you'll get plenty of hits. Most are American but if you want a more British take, try the BBC. When Radio 4's

Today programme interviwed *Smith's* editor, Larry Smith, hundreds of listeners emailed their own six-word life stories, many of which you can still read on the *Today* programme website. Here are a few I particularly liked:

If only I had turned left – Robin Pickering

Ditched the map, found better route – Gillian Smellie

Jennie, Emma, Jane, Sophie, Rose, happiness – Peter Graham

These are all perfect miniature stories in that they depict transition. That was then, this is now; things have changed. Note, too, how each shines a light on a character's attitude to life, one that steers the character on his or her way. The first, for example, depicts regret. The character has an 'if only' attitude, believing that everything would have been better if he'd taken a different path. Contrast this with the last, in which the character goes forward hopefully until he finds the right woman. This character is happy. The first character seems unable to move forward – but there may be hope for him if he looks in another direction. The middle character is feisty, makes her own rules and is not afraid to find alternatives if things aren't working.

Each of these pieces gives the reader something to ponder. All could be developed into longer, more detailed stories. Just ask questions. Take, for example, the character who wished he'd turned left. What was waiting for him in the other direction? Where is he now? Is his story over, or could you introduce an inciting incident to jolt him out of his rut?

Write a story about yourself in just six words. A good tip here is to look for words that act as markers or yardsticks. For example, 'Waiter, chef, restaurateur, own tv show' shows a person's rise to fame from humble beginnings. An 'iceberg' approach, 'Tried greener grass but it withered' hints at a story beneath the waves. If you can do it for yourself, you can do it for a character, and if you write one six-word piece every day, you'll have the kernel of seven characters' stories by the end of the week. Just think of those icebergs beneath the surface. It's enough to get you started on a full-length novel.

Note: At the time of writing, *Smith* magazine is still inviting entries for its 'Six-Word Memoir' project. You can submit at www.smithmag.net/sixwords

Snippet Trigger – The Generous Widow

Here's another snippet trigger, one of those quirky news stories to get you thinking about themes, ideas and plot possibilities. The item appeared on BBC Wales.

> A 90-year-old widow in Wales left £400,000 to her village to thank the residents for their kindness. She and her husband had spent many happy holidays in a small waterfront community and decided to retire there. They stayed for 30 years, joined local clubs and made lots of friends. When the husband died, those friends rallied round. They helped the widow to rebuild her life and looked after her in her final years. She left money to each of them and to many local charities. She also offered £3,000 to anyone who would agree to look after her ginger cat so that he didn't have to go to a cattery.

When you first hear an item like this, it's tempting to think you can turn it into fiction simply by filling it out and adding more detail. Occasionally, that might work but it's not as easy as it looks. In this particular anecdote, for example, the most important information – the punchline, if you like – is at the beginning. If you leave it there, your story is already over. If you move the present beginning to the end, the readers will get bored reading the preamble because there isn't anything there to generate suspense. You'd need to create an alternative narrative to keep things moving. Once you start doing that, you might as well plan a new story, based on the original anecdote, but without its structural constraints.

A better approach is to look for key aspects of the story – themes and ideas that you can develop in a way that suits you and, if you want to sell, your chosen market. You might, for example, see the story as a celebration of karma, the law of moral causation, which states that all actions have consequences that will affect the doer of the action at a future time. If a person does good, for example, that good will eventually be returned to them – although they might have to wait for reincarnation to reap the benefit. In the context of the story, the money left to the villagers was a direct consequence of their earlier kindness to the woman.

Having arrived at the idea of karma, however, you're free to explore it in any way you like. Suppose, for example, the villagers had not been kind? Suppose they had treated the woman as an interloper, gossiped about her, terrorised her cat? It happens. When I discussed this with a friend, his immediate response was to suggest that the woman use the money to pay someone to exact revenge after her death. That's a great idea, and it only took two steps to get there.

Your take on the original story may be completely different. What you see will depend upon your own sensibilities and viewpoint on life. In writing classes, the same trigger always produced an amazing variety of different angles and there is no right or wrong analysis of a piece. What is important is to be open-minded because sometimes the best ideas are hiding under the obvious ones. Try the following exercise.

THE EXERCISE

I've extracted a few themes from the original anecdote. Choose one and do a five-minute freewrite. Alternatively, pull out your own themes and choose one of those.

Karma	Relocation	Love of pets
Rebuilding life after loss	Retirement	Generosity
Friendship	Kindness	Gratitude
Making a will	Happy holidays	Village life

$$17$$

I Probably Shouldn't Be Telling You This But . . .

'You are invited to anonymously contribute a secret to a group art project. Your secret can be a regret, fear, betrayal, desire, confession, or childhood humiliation. Reveal anything – as long as it is true and you have never shared it with anyone before.'

When Frank Warren handed out postcards to strangers, inviting them to contribute their secrets to his community art project, he could not have known how successful it would be. According to the publishers HarperCollins, Warren has now received 150,000 anonymous postcards, many of which have been published in five best-selling books. His website, PostSecret, has won several awards.

What do people reveal? Anything and everything. Some contributions are funny, some shocking and some rather sad, like this one from a selection posted on Mother's Day: *My son told me I was fat so I sent him to his room and ate some of his leftover Easter candy.* Or how about this: *I look inside people's medicine cabinets when I use their bathroom.* I bet that person was a writer.

What can we learn from PostSecret's success? Here are some points to get you thinking about secrets and why they're useful in fiction.

1. The theme of secrets resonates. We all have secrets. Consequently, if you create a character with a secret, you have something that will chime with readers. Secrets arouse curiosity, which is why they appear in so many titles, such as *Can You Keep a Secret?* by Sophie Kinsella, *The Secret Life of Walter Mitty* by James Thurber, and *Harry Potter and the Chamber of Secrets* by J. K. Rowling. When Warner Brothers adapted Elizabeth Goudge's novel *The Little White Horse* for cinema, they changed the title to *The Secret of Moonacre*. Non-fiction, too, gets in on the act, as in the BBC's *The Secret History of our Streets, The Secret Life of Chaos,* and *Secret Britain.*

2. Secrets – if shared with the reader – give the reader a feeling of inclusion. Think about real life. When someone leans over and says, 'Can you keep a secret?' we always say 'yes' even if the first thing we do is pick up the phone and tell someone else. You and I would never do that, of course, but the question is: Why does anybody? It's because the possession of other people's secrets makes us feel special. It gives us something that others might want and that – at base level – is power. 'Secret' societies play the same card. If you belong, you know the secrets. If not, you're an outsider. For any fiction writer, secret societies are a rich source of ideas, even if some of those secrets are inventions, as in Dan Brown's *Da Vinci Code.*

3. Characters with secrets are intriguing. The reader wants to see how the character deals with the secret, what effect the secret has on his/her life, and what decisions the character makes in connection with the secret. As PostSecret's founder, Frank Warren, says: 'You will find your answers in the secrets of strangers.'

4. Secrets are versatile. They work in novels and short stories, and they come in many different flavours: family secrets, embarrassing secrets, delicious secrets, painful secrets, lovers' secrets, shocking secrets, and so on. Many of our best-known writers use secrets in their fiction. In gothic novels, such as

Daphne du Maurier's *Rebecca* and Charlotte Brontë's *Jane Eyre,* the heroes have dark secrets that make it impossible for them to relate to the women they love. In Arthur Conan Doyle's short story *The Man with the Twisted Lip,* Neville St Clair's secret is more humiliating than dark. When he discovers that begging is more profitable than working, he decides to pursue it, but without telling his wife. His sense of shame is his undoing. As he explains to Sherlock Holmes: *'I would have endured imprisonment, ay, even execution, rather than have left my miserable secret as a family blot to my children.'*

THE EXERCISE

◆ To get you into secret mode, freewrite for five minutes using secrets as your theme. Or, if you prefer, do a creative search.

◆ Create five characters, each with a secret. Characters with secrets are more interesting because they reflect real people. Take any shallow character, give him or her a secret and watch that character come to life.

◆ Write about a character who discovers a family secret that changes his or her life. For inspiration, check out the website of best-selling author Kate Morton, who is fascinated by secrets and uses them in all her novels, including *The House at Riverton* and *The Forgotten Garden*, for which she adapted a secret from her own family.

18

Atmospheric Pressure

In Elmore Leonard's *10 Rules of Writing*, the first rule is: *Never open a book with weather*. It's good advice. In fiction, weather isn't interesting – or even relevant – until it affects a character. But when it does, weather has the power to enhance the reader's experience of your story. Here are four reasons you might want to use it.

1. Weather is sensuous. If you write about a chill rain dripping down someone's neck, or a hot wind making your skin itch, the reader will be drawn in at that sensory level. See how Raymond Chandler does it in *Guns at Cyrano's*:

   Ted Malvern liked the rain: liked the feel of it, the sound of it, the smell of it. He got out of his LaSalle coupé and stood for a while by the side entrance to the Carondelet, the high collar of his blue suede huckster tickling his ears, his hands in his pockets and a limp cigarette sputtering between his lips.

   The rain here creates atmosphere but instead of being a gratuitous piece of description, it serves to introduce the reader to Ted Malvern. That 'limp' cigarette is a neat touch.

2. Weather affects mood. We can't do much about that in real life, but in fiction, we can choose whatever weather suits the mood we want to evoke. This helps when trying to elicit an emotional response in the reader or when you want to show a character's emotions. For example, no one who has watched

David Lean's film of *Doctor Zhivago* forgets the bleak
landscape in the scene following the burial of Yuri's mother.
The wind is blowing, snow covers the ground, and the branch
of a tree taps eerily against Yuri's window in the middle of the
night. That scene is lifted straight from the book, where it
serves to symbolise the desolation of the motherless small boy:

> *In just his nightshirt, Yuri ran to the window, and pressed*
> *his face to the cold glass. Beyond the window there was no*
> *road, no cemetery, no kitchen garden. A blizzard was*
> *raging outside; the air was smoky with snow. One might*
> *have thought the storm noticed Yuri, and, knowing how*
> *frightening it was, revelled in the impression it made on*
> *him.*

Yuri is afraid. He fears that the snow, which buried the
cabbages in the kitchen garden, will also bury his mother's
grave and take her even farther away from him. Other writers,
too, have used snow as a symbol of lifelessness and stagnation.
In C. S. Lewis's *The Lion, the Witch and the Wardrobe,* Narnia
is a land frozen in eternal winter, under the rule of the White
Witch. When the children and Aslan defeat the Witch, the
snow and ice melt and spring arrives.

This change of weather here marks not just a change of season
but a change of mood, a rebirth of the kingdom and better
times ahead. It's an easy – but powerful – technique that you
can adapt for your own stories. Build on established
associations or create your own. For example, if magical things
always happen to a character during a fall of snow, readers
will come to associate snow with magic.

3. Weather affects behaviour, which makes it useful for
    characterising people and the places in which they live. In *As
    Good as it Gets,* Simon Nolan uses summer weather to
    characterise Brighton:

Summer came all at once to Brighton. After weeks of dark cloud and unexpectedly cold winds, one day there were blue skies, heat, people in T-shirts and cut-offs, sweat and booming open-top cars full of ravers with non-specific expressions of pleasure plastered over their faces.

Remember, too, that a particular character's feelings and opinions about weather give insight into their personality. In the extract from *Guns at Cyrano's,* Ted Malvern likes the rain. Charlotte Brontë's Jane Eyre has a different perspective:

There was no possibility of taking a walk that day. We had been wandering, indeed, in the leafless shrubbery an hour in the morning; but since dinner (Mrs. Reed, when there was no company, dined early) the cold winter wind had brought with it clouds so sombre, and a rain so penetrating, that further out-door exercise was now out of the question. I was glad of it: I never liked long walks, especially on chilly afternoons: dreadful to me was the coming home in the raw twilight, with nipped fingers and toes . . .

4. Weather makes an effective plotting device. In *Storm of the Century*, Stephen King uses a hurricane and five feet of snow to maroon the residents of Tall Island while the evil Linoge does his dirty work. In the Batman film *The Dark Knight Rises*, the city is frozen, both literally and metaphorically. Extreme weather threatens the characters just as much as the nuclear bomb. Classic literature may be short on bombs but writers like Thomas Hardy and Jane Austen were big fans of weather. In *Pride and Prejudice*, for example, Elizabeth is detained at Pemberley after catching cold during a rainstorm. This gives her plenty of opportunities to fraternise with Mr Darcy.

Using weather as a plot device might seem contrived but weather has always played a significant role in our lives, shaping everything from the village fete to the destiny of nations. Two fascinating books, *Blame it on the Rain* by Laura Lee and *The Weather Factor: How Nature has changed History* by Erik Durschmied, explore the implication of weather in world events. For example, in 1845, weather-induced blight ruined the Irish potato harvest, causing famine. One million people died and another million left the country, some for North America, others for towns and cities in England and Scotland. This changed the demographic of such places for ever. On a less epic scale, storms can prevent us from reaching our destinations, bring down power cables, and create all sorts of problems for aircraft trying to land on inhospitable terrain.

THE EXERCISE

◆ Use weather as the focus of a creative search. We've talked about rain, snow, sun, wind and storms, but what about fog, clouds, hurricanes and tornadoes? Any one of these options might be just the trigger you need for a story.

◆ Create some situations in which weather affects a character, or characters. For example, a fresh fall of snow might hide a murderer's tracks, a flash flood might maroon the inhabitants of a village. Choose one of your situations to explore in more detail.

◆ Take a scene in one of your stories and see how changing the season affects the mood. Would your scene work better in hot sunshine, rain or perhaps even a thunderstorm? Add a few sensory details: the smell of bonfires, the ping of hail on the roof of a car, the squelch of mud underfoot. Experiment.

19

Make Them Smile

When Tracy Chevalier judged the Bridport Short Story Prize she was disappointed to find so little humour in the entries. Most of the stories, she said, made her depressed: 'While I'm not in a position to chastise – I myself am not known for many laughs in my books – I would like to make a plea to future writers: humour is good!'

Unfortunately, it seems no one was listening because, three years later, judge Zoë Heller said much the same thing: 'This year's writers experimented with all sorts of tones and moods – brutal, meditative, grim, melancholy, wistful, whimsical, erotic – but very few of them took the risk of striking a comic note.' She added: 'Please take heed ... making a reader laugh does not compromise your claim to being taken seriously as a writer of literary fiction.'

In the mass market, a dash of humour is even more important. People buy magazines as a treat, something to read while having a coffee. If you can make an editor smile, you're on to a winner. Smiling releases endorphins – 'feel good' chemicals – in the brain that can help lower stress levels. My first successful short story sold on its humour. The editor said it made her laugh. Another plus for humour – it never goes out of fashion. 'Humour is always welcome,' says Gaynor Davies, Fiction Editor of *Woman's Weekly*.

But how can we incorporate humour into our fiction? I asked myself that question when I was trying to break into print. I'm not a life-and-soul-of-the-party type. If I tell a joke, not only have you probably heard it before but I frequently mess up the punchline – or completely forget it. My solution was to look at the authors who made me smile and see how they did it. I discovered that, despite their differences, they had one technique in common. They used metaphorical language – similes and metaphors – to create vivid images. Just to clarify, a simile is a figure of speech in which one thing is compared to another, using a comparison word such as 'like' or 'as'. A metaphor simply dispenses with the comparison word. For example, 'The moon looks *like* a pockmarked cheese' is a simile. 'The moon *is* a pockmarked cheese' is a metaphor.

Metaphorical language is not funny in itself. *He was a tubby little chap whose clothes fitted like a second skin* contains a simile – 'like a second skin' – but it isn't funny. By contrast, *He was a tubby little chap who looked as if he had been poured into his clothes and had forgotten to say 'when'* is funny. The latter is from P. G. Wodehouse, who loved to beef up his similes with exaggeration and absurdity. Here are a few of my personal favourites:

◆ *Her face was shining like the seat of a bus-driver's trousers.*

◆ *Jeeves lugged my purple socks out of the drawer as if he were a vegetarian fishing a caterpillar out of his salad.*

◆ *He paused, and swallowed convulsively, like a Pekingese taking a pill.*

If you want to introduce humour into your work, Wodehouse is one of the best authors to study. Hugh Laurie, who played Bertie Wooster in the television adaptation of *Jeeves and Wooster* describes Wodehouse as 'the funniest writer ever to have put words on paper'. He cheers people up. Numerous *Desert Island Disc* castaways, including Rowan Atkinson, Richard Dawkins and the journalist Anne Leslie, all chose a Wodehouse book to take with them to the island.

So, what characteristics of Wodehouse's metaphorical language can you use in your own writing? While Wodehouse's work is unique, there are features of it that lend themselves readily to adaptation. Here are three for you to try out.

1. Animal imagery. Wodehouse loved to compare people, and aspects of people, to animals. Bertie's Aunt Agatha is *like an elephant– not so much to look at, for in appearance she resembles more a well-bred vulture, but because she never forgets.* His friend Tuppy *somewhat resembles a bulldog, and his aspect now was that of one of these fine animals who has just been refused a slice of cake.*

2. A new twist on cliché. Wodehouse used plenty of tired expressions in his writing but he always revitalised them by adding an extra, unexpected twist. For example, *I'd always thought her half-baked, but now I think they didn't even put her in the oven.* Or: *He trusted neither of them as far as he could spit, and he was a poor spitter, lacking both distance and control.* An easy way to introduce a form of this technique into your own work is to take a cliché, such as 'You could have knocked me over with a feather' and swap 'feather' for another word – one that fits the context of your own story better. For example, if your story were set in a biscuit factory, you might say 'You could have knocked me over with a chocolate digestive.' Or, if your main character is a florist: 'You could have knocked me over with a sweet pea posy.' OK, so it's not quite Wodehouse, but I promise you it works because I've used it myself.

3. Hyperbole. Hyperbole is just a fancy term for exaggeration. It's a defining feature of Wodehouse's work and often appears in extended metaphors and similes. For example: *I turned to Aunt Agatha, whose demeanour was now rather like that of one who, picking daisies on the railway, has just caught the down express in the small of the back.*

There is obviously a lot more to Wodehouse's humour than metaphorical language, but it is an intrinsic part. I chose the above features because they're readily transferable and many other writers have used them to good effect. For example, in the television series *Blackadder Goes Forth,* Captain Blackadder employs animal imagery to describe the lack of progress at the front: *Millions have died, but our troops have advanced no further than an asthmatic ant with some heavy shopping.* Jilly Cooper often uses animal imagery to create amusing word pictures of her characters: *He reminded Sophie of a knowing old Scottie dog, just back from the butcher's with a large bone and sawdust hanging from his fur tummy.* Garrison Keillor revitalises tired expressions: *She hasn't just got a screw loose – the whole lid's blown off.* And Raymond Chandler's work is an herbaceous border of hyperbole and extended metaphor: *I'm an occasional drinker, the kind of guy who goes out for a beer and wakes up in Singapore with a full beard.* I also love this snatch of dialogue from the film *Romancing the Stone*: *'You don't want to go to Colombia. They have insects there the size of sanitation trucks.'*

Now, it's over to you. Try the following exercise.

THE EXERCISE

Choose one of the following options.

◆ Create a character, or more than one if you have time, and describe the character(s) using animal imagery.

◆ Rewrite the following clichés, adding an extra twist and/or hyperbole if you like.
  − You could have knocked me over with a feather.
  − It was like talking to a brick wall.
  − A bird in the hand is worth two in the bush.
  − It was the best thing since sliced bread.

◆ Fill in the blanks in the following sentences, using one or more features of Wodehouse style:
  − When the morning mail arrived, he sprang out of bed like _____
  − She smoothed her hair with a nervous gesture like _____
  − His jaw fell like _____
  − He was as angry as a _____
  − She felt dazed and confused as if she had been _____
  − She had a pale face and hair that always looked like _____
  − His expression changed. Before, he could have been mistaken for a shark about to bite. His air now was that of a _____

20

The Tiffany Window of Desire

Are you having trouble bringing one of your characters to life? Perhaps you need to create a new character and are wondering where to start. Or perhaps you're looking for a way to reveal aspects of your character in scenes guaranteed to strike a chord with your readers. Shops and shopping might just be your answer.

In one of cinema's most iconic opening scenes, Audrey Hepburn gazes into the window of Tiffany & Co., jewellers on Fifth Avenue, New York. It's early morning. She's eating a Danish. The film is *Breakfast at Tiffany's* – from the book by Truman Capote. For Holly Golightly, Hepburn's character, Tiffany's is more than just a posh store full of jewellery she can't afford. Holly is single, flitting from party to party and man to man, all the time yearning for stability. Tiffany's, with its traditionalism, its quiet and its dreamlike interior, is her Shangri-la: 'I don't want to own anything until I find a place where me and things go together,' she says. 'I'm not sure where that is but I know what it is like. It's like Tiffany's, the best place in the world, where nothing bad can take place.'

Throughout the book, Capote uses Holly's frequent references to Tiffany's to highlight the contrast between her precarious real life and the security she craves. Three decades later, in the film *Pretty Woman*, the writers used a scene in a Rodeo Drive fashion house to highlight a similar contrast between Vivienne's life as a hooker and the affluent elite to which she aspires. Unlike Holly, Vivienne enters the store, where the snobby assistants humiliate her. Later, in the now-famous shopping scene, Edward insists on spending an 'obscene' amount of money on new designer clothes for her, thus marking her entry into 'the fairy tale'. For both Holly and Vivienne, posh shops are not just places selling goods. They are psychological gateways to new identities.

Which brings us to a character whose identity, constructed of daredevil exploits and designer labels, has become a global phenomenon. The character is James Bond and, yes, he does go shopping. Take a look at this:

> *The drug-store first for half a dozen of Owens incomparable toothbrushes. Hoffritz on Madison Avenue for one of their heavy, toothed Gillette-type razors ... Triplers for some of those French golf socks made by Izod, Scribner's because it was the last great bookshop in New York and because there was a salesman there with a good nose for thrillers, and then to Abercrombie's to look over the new gadgets ...*

The above extract, from a short story entitled *007 in New York,* points up the brand-laden construction of Bond, whose appetites for fast cars, fast women and even faster storylines have delighted the public for over half a century. What Fleming understood, as did the authors of the later sex 'n' shopping novels, is that the seductive power of luxury brands is to do with aspiration. In the 1950s, when Bond arrived, ordinary people were not big spenders; most had never even been abroad. Consequently, when Bond strode into the arena, flashing his Rolex, his Aston Martin, and a taste for beluga caviar, readers (and filmgoers) had vicarious entry into an impossibly glamorous and sophisticated world. What Bond offered – still offers – is a series of 'tiffany' windows through which we can see our own fantasies reflected. There is now even a website, jamesbondlifestyle, which gives details of his clothes, gadgets, food, drink and travel destinations.

As research for this exercise, I asked students to imagine themselves on their favourite shopping street with cash in their pocket. What would they buy? One woman came up with all the usual things, a nice car, some Italian shoes, and so on. 'But really,' she said, 'it's not so much what I would buy, but what I *could* buy if I wanted to. It's the security of not having to worry about things, if you know what I mean?' I did indeed know what she meant. We're back to the calm, ordered world behind Tiffany's window where nothing bad can ever happen – but if it does, James Bond will deal with it.

In real life, we are all revealed by what we buy and what we desire – even the things we can't afford. Consequently, in fiction, shops and shopping scenes offer limitless opportunities to say something about your character. Sophie Kinsella even has a whole series of *Shopaholic* novels about a character called Becky Bloomwood whose addiction to shopping creates problems at every turn.

Shopping also creates problems in *The Family Man,* a film starring Nicolas Cage as a Wall Street executive, Jack, who wakes up one Christmas to find himself living in a parallel universe. His Ferrari and jet-setting lifestyle have vanished, replaced by a loving wife, Kate, two children and a job in a tyre shop. At the local mall, Jack tries on a suit that he can only afford by raiding the children's college fund. The scene points up the conflict within Jack as he tries to reconcile the advantages of being part of a loving family with what he sees as the humiliation of being poor. Kate asks him to take the suit off. Jack refuses. The suit, he says, makes him 'feel like a better person'. Kate is bewildered and suggests they go to the food court to 'get some of that funnel cake you like'.

The stark contrast between the expensive suit and the funnel cake highlights the different values of the two characters. For non-materialistic Kate, a treat is pancakes with maple syrup on Christmas morning with the children. For Jack, an expensive suit makes him feel like a 'better person' – a poignant comment on the 21st-century notion that our self-worth is defined by the products we buy. It's a film well worth watching.

THE EXERCISE

To explore the idea of shops and shopping, use one of the following as inspiration.

◆ Fantasy spending. A distant relation has left you £1,000 to spend on whatever you want. You cannot save it or give it away. What would you buy?

◆ You are a private detective who has been asked to find out as much as you can about a particular character. You decide to shadow the character on a shopping trip. Choose a street you know, and (in your imagination!) follow the character from one end to the other. Where does the character shop? What does s/he buy? Write a short piece detailing what you have discovered about the character, based on their buying choices.

◆ Write a short scene set in a shop. Your goal is to highlight the differences between two characters, as in *The Family Man.* You could invent the characters from scratch or, if you prefer, you can use something from your own experience. For example, I recently went into Jolly's department store in Bath to buy a lipstick. The assistant was busy with another customer who seemed to be buying everything she was offered. 'Would you like some serum to go with that?' Oh, yes, she would. 'And how about some of this blemish balm. It's full of antioxidants...' This went on for another ten minutes. Her bill came to £150. As I left the store with my single lipstick, I had a sneaking suspicion that she had a drawer full of other cosmetics that she never used.

$$\boxed{21}$$

Who's Got the Power?

One of my most popular workshops explores the dynamics of power in stories. When a person has power – or perceives themselves as having power – it affects their behaviour. Perhaps the most striking example of this is the famous Stanford prison experiment, in which college students were assigned the role of either prisoner or guard in a mock prison setting. These roles influenced the participants' behaviour to such an extent that the experiment had to be stopped. The 'guards', heady with newly acquired power, became sadistic, while the 'prisoners' became so cowed and stressed that some had to be treated for depression.

But what exactly is power and how can we use it in our fiction? Power is simply a person's ability to influence others. French and Raven, two social psychologists interested in group dynamics, identified five different types. Later, Hershey and Blanchard, two management gurus who applied the model to business negotiation, added two more. For writers, an understanding of these different powers can enhance our ability to create dynamic scenes and eliminate 'dead' space. Power is central to conflict, in which power clashes often lead to power shift. An obvious example of this shift occurs at the climax of thrillers when the hero finally succeeds in defeating the baddie. Identifying different characters' sources of power also helps to deepen our understanding of those characters and their motivations.

Let's start by listing the different types of power, with some examples.

1. LEGITIMATE POWER

This is power which comes from a character's position or status. A detective uses legitimate power when he detains suspects and questions them. So does a lollipop lady when she stops traffic to allow children to cross the road. Motorists allow her to do this because it's her job. Legitimate power is easy to recognise in fiction. In Joanne Harris's *Chocolat,* Father Reynaud uses his status as a Catholic priest to keep villagers away from Vianne's new chocolate shop. In the television series *Merlin,* Arthur's power comes from his status as both a king and a respected knight of Camelot. His power is very different from that of Merlin, who, in this particular adaptation of Arthurian legend, is a servant. Merlin's power belongs in the next category.

2. EXPERT POWER

Expert power comes from having superior knowledge or a useful skill. Unlike King Arthur, Merlin's status is lowly. His power comes from his ability to perform magic, which he has to keep secret because sorcery is illegal. As a result, the power dynamic between Arthur and Merlin is often comic, with Arthur chiding Merlin for incompetence, only to have Merlin saving his life without his realising it.

Almost any kind of skill or knowledge can endow a character with expert power, provided the character uses it to achieve something. For example, Archibald Mulliner, a P. G. Wodehouse character, has one talent, the ability to give an imitation of a chicken laying an egg. He uses this to woo the girl of his dreams. In the film *Pretty Woman,* Vivienne, a street prostitute, displays expert power when Edward asks her for directions to Beverley Hills. Their dialogue exchange is a great example of that shift in power I mentioned earlier. Vivienne says that it will cost him. Edward, a rich man driving a Ferrari, argues that she can't charge for giving directions. Vivienne retorts: 'I can charge whatever I want. I'm not lost.'

Vivienne has another more obvious source of power, which we'll look at next.

3. REWARD POWER

This is the power to give others something they want or value. It could be sex, money, love or even a smile. Parents use this power when they say to a child: 'If you're good, I'll read you a story/give you a biscuit/ let you stay up late...' In the television series *Dad's Army*, Corporal Jones, the town butcher, uses this power to get what he wants. At a time of meat rationing, Jones's sausages are a luxury which Captain Mainwaring cannot resist.

4. COERCIVE POWER

Coercive power is based on threat, punishment or suppression of free will. Dick Turpin uses coercive power when he tells travellers 'Your money or your life.' Charles Dickens's novels are full of characters who resort to coercive power. Fagin makes boys pick pockets in return for food and a roof over their heads. Scrooge expects his clerk to work all hours under threat of losing his job. In Ian Fleming's *Casino Royale,* the scene in which James Bond is stripped, tied to a chair and beaten to make him talk is a classic example of coercive power. Most Bond books – indeed most thrillers – contain a few such scenes and the sixty-four-thousand-dollar question is always 'How will the hero get out of this one?' We, of course, would ask, 'Which power will s/he use?'

5. REFERENT OR PERSONAL ATTRIBUTE POWER

This power comes from a person's attractiveness to others. Celebrities have referent power, which is why advertising agencies use them to promote everything from hair products to car insurance. It's a staple power in romantic fiction, but also in literature, where good looks are sometimes associated with other less worthy characteristics. In Thomas Hardy's *Far from the Madding Crowd,* Sergeant Troy is a charming bounder whose shortcomings a lovesick Bathsheba overlooks. By contrast, the good but dull Gabriel Oak, who knows everything about sheep farming, has expert power. Bathsheba goes to him for help and advice, and eventually realises that he is the better man.

6. CONNECTION POWER

This is the 'it's-not-what-you-know-but-who-you-know' power which comes from a person's association with another, more influential individual. We all know people who love to name-drop. 'I bumped into Liz today – that's Liz Hurley, not the Queen, I'm not that grand – ha-ha-ha . . .'

When people feel vulnerable, they often reach for connection power. For example, in a television drama I heard an elderly character say: 'My son's collecting me. He's an accountant, you know.' This latter fact was irrelevant, so why mention it? Partly pride in her son, of course, but also because in her declining years her son's achievements were a source of her own self-esteem.

In the film *Romancing the Stone*, novelist Joan Wilder is out of her comfort zone in the wilds of Colombia. First, she uses reward power ($375) to persuade jungle-savvy Jack Colton to help her reach Cartagena. A neat power shift occurs when they try to hire a car and local men threaten them with guns. 'OK, Joan Wilder,' says Jack. 'Write us out of this one.' At which point, one of the men cries 'Joan *Wilder*! You are Joan Wilder?' It turns out he's a big fan, has all her books and offers to lend them his truck. Jack then has to rely on his connection to Joan, while Joan's writing talent gets them out of trouble. This rebalances the power dynamic between the two characters.

7. INFORMATION OR ACCESS POWER

Information power comes from an individual's ability to access information. In fiction, we might see this as 'gatekeeper' power. In the television series *Doc Martin,* for example, the receptionist has all the patient records on a database, plus the results of tests, and the appointments diary. Like all receptionists, she has the power to reveal or conceal, to allow or to block. In the Sherlock Holmes stories, Dr Watson has information power. His understanding of Holmes's methods and his cases enables him to liaise with clients when Holmes is unavailable.

Paul Elsam, whose book *Acting Characters* using the French and Raven model to teach aspiring actors to prepare for their role, points out that an awareness of the different types of power can help to 'clarify why your character behaves the way he does, and why others allow him to do so'. For writers, who must create characters and plotlines from scratch, posing questions about each character's source(s) of power can generate ideas. A character might be strong on one type of power, but weak in another. You can exploit this imbalance to maximise dramatic potential. In the Jeeves and Wooster stories, for example, Jeeves is a valet whose main power is his extraordinary ability to find solutions to Bertie Wooster's problems. As his employer – and a rich man to boot – Bertie might be expected to have all types of power at his disposal. In fact, his main power source is his connection to

Jeeves, who can solve Bertie's friends' problems, too. This is a neat reversal of the usual situation and makes for great comedy.

THE EXERCISE

◆ To get you thinking about how power functions in the real world, list some people from your own life. What sources of power do they use? Remember that our sources of power vary according to context. Children, for example, who are adept users of all seven, may use connection power at school: 'My dad's bigger than your dad' – and reward power at home: 'Dad, if I tidy my room, will you buy me a hamster?'

◆ Take a favourite television series, list the characters and see if you can identify their sources of power. I've already mentioned Corporal Jones in *Dad's Army*, but the other major characters have their own sources of power. These all interact to create great comedy.

◆ Write a scene in which a character uses one specific type of power to influence another. What type of power does the other character use? Remember, nobody is ever completely without power. Even in the direst situation, there is always something for which a person can reach.

Snippet Trigger – The Sexy Isle

When the Ann Summers chain once named its Isle of Man store
as the top-achieving store of the month, the manager was
delighted. 'The store's success is proof of its huge popularity on
the island,' she told *Isle of Man Today*. 'And we think it shows just
how sexy a population the Isle of Man people really are.'
According to sales figures, the most popular item of the month (it
was December) included a Mrs Santa outfit and a pilot outfit.

Well, it makes a change from the TT races, Manx cats, and the
Lady Isabella, otherwise known as the Laxey Wheel. Or could
they all be connected? I like the idea of a Laxey resident getting
on the phone to her friend in Port Erin: 'Audrey, you know I told
you that Lady Isabella next door was having an affair? Yes, I was
putting Monty out for his constitutional and I saw a pilot
skulking in the rhododendrons. Well, I've just read the paper and
...I think it might have been George dressed up. I *know*. First the
motorbike, now this.'

For writers, looking for connections between unlikely things is a
tried-and-tested method of sparking a story, and when one of
those items is sex, how can you lose? While the Isle of Man may
not be the first setting that comes to mind, it's certainly seen a lot
of action in its time. Steeped in Viking history, it's full of
mountains, glens, rushing water, wild scenery, and secluded
beaches. It also has a couple of castles, one of which, Castle
Rushen, boasts a drawbridge and – in the inner gatehouse –

murder holes through which heavy stones, hot sand, molten lead or boiling tar could be dropped to deter invaders. Sex and the Island? Why not? Candace Bushnell did pretty well out of her *Sex and the City* column, based on her own experiences of dating in New York. It's a different world now, and while elegance will never die, bling has given way to putting on wellies, keeping hens and growing runner beans.

Your take on the piece may of course be very different from mine – and that's just as it should be. A snippet trigger is like an open box, full of options. You take what you want, and throw away what you don't. It often helps to consider the points of view of characters not mentioned in the original story. For example, how might the story affect nearby businesses? Suppose there's an empty shop next door that used to be a family cafe? And so on.

Try the following exercise.

THE EXERCISE

◆ Do a five-minute creative search, using 'sex' as your trigger.

◆ To explore some connections, take two of the following Manx-inspired items and combine them with sex to create an idea for a story.

Island	Myths and legends	Cat
Medieval castle	Sea	Waterwheel
Fairy folklore (e.g. Fairy Bridge)	Mist	Mountain
Motorbike	Thatched cottage	Millionaire
Viking longboat	Deserted beach	Woollen mill

Alternatively, choose a place that's familiar to you, and use items from that.

23

Lucky Dip Bag

Not so much an exercise, more a lifesaver when your creative brain has gone AWOL, the lucky dip bag is a writing class staple. Its principle is simple. You write ideas on bits of card and pop them into the bag. Over time, the cards accumulate and when you need a writing trigger the bag will oblige.

In writing classes, we don't have a permanent bag of triggers. I usually suggest a category, such as 'beautiful objects' or 'a snatch of dialogue' just for that evening. Once everyone has put their contribution into the bag, we pass the bag around a second time for people to dip and pull out a card. It's fun working from a classmate's trigger, and students also find it interesting to hear what someone else has made of their contribution. Sometimes, we pull two cards and the challenge then is to write a piece that combines both. What, for example, could you do with: *He told me not to tell anyone* and *This fish has gone off*?

Combining two triggers works because the brain will always search for connections and pattern even when there is nothing obvious to be found. It's a bit like those join-the-dots pictures in children's puzzle books – or the chicken nugget that sold for £5,000 on eBay because it 'resembled' the face of George Washington.

Although the lucky dip bag is popular in workshop groups, one advantage of working alone is that you can tailor the contents to suit you. Some writers, for example, like single-word triggers, while others prefer a little more detail. Feel free to experiment and see what works best for you. The process has the pleasant feel of ritual about it and there's also an element of serendipity. If you didn't consciously choose the card, perhaps the card chose you?

THE EXERCISE

First, find a bag, and a supply of small cards or even pieces of paper, just big enough to contain a few words. I use a red fabric drawstring bag that once contained airline goodies, but you can use whatever you have to hand. I know one writer who uses an old shoebox with a slot cut in the top to post the cards into. Now, make yourself a 'float' of cards. Later, you may decide to have several different bags, each containing a specific category, such as characters, places and objects, which you can mix and match to suit yourself. In the meantime, here are some categories to get you started on a mixed bag.

◆ Single words. The easiest way to find a single word is to open your dictionary and stick in a pin.

◆ Colours. This might seem like an unlikely category but one writer assures me that writing about different colours gives her ideas. You can have the basic colours, red, yellow and blue, etc., but how about 'moss green', 'periwinkle' or 'terracotta'?

◆ A few words of dialogue. You can dream up your own dialogue or open a novel and find some that take your fancy.

◆ Names. When you hear someone's name do you start to form a picture of the person in your mind? Geraldine Wintherbotham just isn't the same as Lily Conrad. Names are evocative, even when they're fictional. This makes them useful triggers for a five-minute writing burst, with the added chance that you may end up with a brand-new character. Find surnames in the telephone directory and add a first name.

24

A Pram in the Hall

'There is no more sombre enemy of good art than the pram in the hall,' wrote Cyril Connolly in 1938. As a literary critic, Connolly coined many pithy aphorisms, and this one has ruffled a lot of feathers in recent years. For some, it's misogynistic rubbish, for others, an insightful observation. Reportedly, it even influenced the singer Jarvis Cocker's decision to delay parenthood.

For fiction writers, anything that has the power to arouse strong feelings, arguments and counter-arguments is worth a closer look. I was particularly struck by Andrew Clover's take on the topic. In a *Sunday Times* article entitled 'That pram in the hall isn't the enemy, it's my greatest inspiration', Clover talks about his own reluctance to have children. He was, he says, initially worried that fatherhood would change his life and stop him doing the things he enjoyed, like going to the pub. And he was right – at least about the pub. But, there were compensations. Instead of spoiling his life, his two girls taught him to see it in a new light. They introduced him to lift-the-flap books, to waving at trains, and gathering red leaves with brown lines from the tree outside the pub. They reminded him of many things he used to enjoy. And as for Cyril Connolly?

I think Cyril Connolly lost his creativity, because he left that pram in the hall. He could have pushed it to the park. He could have got in himself, and watched the falling leaves. Or he could have watched his children. They are more beautiful, even, than the red leaves with brown lines.

Andrew Clover's piece is a wonderful example of how there are always other ways to look at the landscape of our lives. For Connolly, the 'enemy' pram in the hall was an obstacle or barrier to his creativity. For Clover, it became an opportunity to see the world through a different window. And through that window was a view that not only changed his mind about having children but gave him fresh insight into creativity.

Although Clover's piece is not fiction, it taps into the heart of what fiction is about. Fiction shows characters engaging with their problems, searching out paths that lead to change and enlightenment. Although the journey may be rough, that's part of the deal. Clover's path, which takes him from fear of fatherhood (the problem) through engagement with it and finally to joy is a perfect example of how a plotline works in terms of transition. If you can keep that progression in mind you won't fall into the trap of writing stories that are static. Your characters will have learned something and emerge as different people as a result of what they have experienced on their journey.

Remember to show the reader what happened to bring about the transition. Clover takes care to detail the little things his girls taught him about recovering the lost joys of childhood. This allows us, the readers, to accompany him on the journey. We may not have made the same decision as he did, but that doesn't matter. A story does not tell its readers how to live – it shows them how someone else handled a situation, the path he chose and where the path led.

We all have our own 'prams in the hall', things we try to avoid because they're too risky or too scary. We can apply the metaphor to any situation in our lives, particularly those that involve bold choices with potentially life-changing consequences. It doesn't have to be about children, but families – your own and those of other people – are a good source of ideas. For example, I've just been reading about families who've decided that the best way to cope with shrinking incomes is for parents, children and grandparents to move in together. That's a huge leap into the unknown, one which few would have contemplated a few years ago, when everyone wanted to do their own thing. Now, it's an option with lots of challenges and opportunities for growth.

If family is not your style, then how about Rachel Khoo, who went to Paris to learn to cook and then decided to open a restaurant in her own apartment? Starting any business is a risky move, but when the apartment is a studio, and the bed has to be folded up before any cooking can begin, it sounds like madness. It was a leap of faith but it worked. Diners loved the intimacy of the one-table restaurant and the food was good, too. Khoo later had her own television series, *The Little Paris Kitchen.*

Sometimes the only way to find out if a decision is the right one is to take the risk of its being wrong. Wheel the pram out and see what happens.

THE EXERCISE

Choose one of the following options:

◆ Do a creative search using 'family' as your trigger or, if you prefer, do a freewrite. We all have families and every family has its challenges, its sources of happiness and sadness. Look for the 'prams in the hall', the difficult situations where a change in viewpoint might be the answer, but for which there is no guarantee that things will work out.

◆ Think about your own life and the things you'd like to do but don't because of obstacles. Maybe you, like Rachel Khoo, had a dream of doing something, but never got around to it. In fiction, you can. What are your personal 'prams in the hall'? Write for five minutes.

We Are What We Eat

The *Observer* newspaper once ran a series entitled 'What's in your basket?' Various celebrities, including writers, musicians and actors, gave a potted history of their eating habits and favourite foods, after which a doctor assessed how healthy their diets were. As you might guess, the results were a touch predictable and obvious. Barbara Taylor Bradford's tinned custard was deemed 'too sugary' to be healthy, Lynne Truss's fruit pastilles were a 'dental hazard' and might induce 'surges of insulin'. As for dancer Darcey Bussell's fondness for frankfurters – all that salt and fat – the doc was appalled.

Rather more interesting for writers was the series' insight into the contributors' lives, their routines and rituals. Take breakfast, for example. Everyone has their own unique approach that somehow suits their persona. For example, I wasn't surprised to learn that the throaty-voiced actor John Hurt starts his day with a whole cafetière of strong black coffee. The literary novelist William Boyd prefers tea, which he has with toast and the juice of four oranges, extracted with a manual squeezer. It is, he says, the same breakfast he's had for the past 20 years. By contrast ex-SAS hero Andy McNab grabs food on the go: 'I get up and make a cup of tea and pick up a banana or something and fold it between a slice of bread.' He doesn't eat lunch, either, although he sometimes pops into Starbucks or Pret A Manger for a baguette.

McNab's routine sounds a bit like that of his famous character, Nick Stone, give or take a few Mars bars – which is perhaps not surprising since Nick Stone is also ex-SAS. Here he is in *Deep Black*:

> *The toast popped up. I went and shoved a fresh batch of cheese squares between the unbuttered slices and scraped the last bit of Branston from the jar with a dirty teaspoon. I'd been getting through three or four jars of the stuff a week. Ezra would have had a field day if I'd told him: I clearly had an unfulfilled longing for the old country.*

Although food makes a useful pacing device between more action-packed content, the above extract shows it can be far more. The food people buy, when and how they choose to eat it, are as much a part of their character as how they speak. And because we can all relate to food, scenes in which characters eat resonate with readers. At the Bath Literature Festival, William Boyd talked about looking for 'that one detail that radiates the page'. A good example, he says, occurs in James Joyce's *Ulysses* where Leopold Bloom goes into Davy Byrnes pub on Duke Street in Dublin and orders a glass of Burgundy and a Gorgonzola cheese sandwich with mustard. The scene that follows is laden with taste, texture and a feeling of ritual:

> *Mr Bloom ate his strips of sandwich, fresh clean bread, with relish of disgust, pungent mustard, the feety savour of green cheese. Sips of his wine soothed his palate. Not logwood that. Tastes fuller this weather with the chill off. Nice quiet bar. Nice piece of wood in that counter. Nicely planed. Like the way it curves there.*

How wonderfully idiosyncratic – with the added advantage that Joyce didn't have to go far for his research. He was himself one of Davy Byrnes' regulars. Today, Davy Byrnes is on the Dublin literary tourist trail and you can still buy the famous Gorgonzola sandwich.

According to screenwriter and director Nancy Meyers, the visual aspect of food makes it a useful tool for creating and controlling mood. She cites *It's Complicated,* a film in which her main character (played by Meryl Streep) is a baker: 'When you see Meryl Streep's character baking at 5a.m., it makes you happy. But when you see her weeding the vegetable garden, you know she's sad.' It's a classic example of show, don't tell.

Remember, too, that irrespective of individual differences every culture has its own traditions and customs relating to food and drink, which can help you out when you're trying to convey the character of a place. Think of the Japanese tea ceremony, with its focus on tranquillity, harmony and respect; American Thanksgiving, with its pumpkin pie; or the French insistence on fresh baguettes every day. If you've ever watched *Indiana Jones and the Temple of Doom*, you'll remember the culinary horrors of the banquet in Pankot Palace. Snake surprise (the snakes are alive), sheep's-eye soup and – for dessert – chilled monkey brains. Yummy yummy. It's a great scene and very funny as Willie (Indiana's sidekick) gets more and more desperate for some proper food.

And finally, let's end as we started, with breakfast. In Nevil Shute's classic novel, *A Town Like Alice,* London secretary Jean Paget goes to Queensland in search of an Australian soldier she met when they were both prisoners of war in Malaya. This is

1940s outback Australia, the weather is sweltering, and Jean cannot stomach the hotel breakfast of half a pound of steak with two fried eggs on top. But there's a problem. When she asks the waitress for one egg and no steak, the waitress reminds her that breakfast is steak and eggs:

> *'I know it is,' said Jean. 'But I don't want the steak.'*
>
> *'Well, you don't have to eat it.' The girl was obviously puzzled.*
>
> *'Couldn't I have just one fried egg and no steak?' asked Jean.*
>
> *'You mean just one fried egg on a plate by itself?'*
>
> *'That's right.'*
>
> *Food conversation in Willstown was evidently quite a new idea. 'I'll ask Mrs Connor,' said Annie. She came back from the kitchen with a steak and two fried eggs on top. 'We've only got the one breakfast,' she explained. Jean gave up the struggle.*

Although the breakfast highlights the difference between Jean's tastes and those of the local people, the scene isn't really about food. It's there to foreshadow potential problems between Jean's lifestyle and that of outback culture. Joe Harmon, the man for whom she's searching, is part of that culture. How will Jean, with her London ways and her liking for lipstick and nice clothes, cope? Is their relationship doomed before it begins? It's a powerful scene, and all made possible by different attitudes to breakfast.

Try the following exercise.

◆ Think about your own breakfast routine. What does it reveal about you, your family, your culture? Write for five minutes.

◆ Create a breakfast routine for a fictional character. Imagine how you would show this on film. Now, write your piece, using the visual aspect of the routine to show the character to a reader. Feel free to use brand names and specific details of the products. For example, if your character has bread, is it brown, white, soda or maybe even an artisan sourdough? Does your character drink out of a mug or a cup? Tea leaves or tea bags?

Note: For another exercise involving food, try Exercise 3 in 'The Nostalgic Tastebud'.

26

Lassoing the Reader

When I was a child I watched a lot of Westerns and one thing they all had in common was the lasso. This iconic piece of cowboy equipment is just a long rope with a running noose at one end. Throw it around a horse, a calf, or even a person, and they're stopped in their tracks. Much as we might like to, we can't use a literal lasso to stop our readers disappearing into the sunset – or even the nearest bar. But we can still learn from classic genre fiction techniques.

J. G. Cawelti, whose love of popular literature led to a lifelong academic study of it, emphasises the importance of encouraging the reader to identify with the main character. In genre fiction, that's a challenge. First, the narrative emphasis is on action; if that stops, the story stalls. Also, main characters often have little in common with normal people: 'They are heroes who have the strength and courage to overcome great dangers, lovers who find perfectly-suited partners, inquirers of exceptional brilliance who discover hidden truths.' Genre fiction copes by using a simple but emotionally based style that forges immediate involvement in a character's actions without the need for psychological complexity. Let's take a look at how to achieve this:

[Aquarius (Jan 20–Feb 19) A difficult day. You will face varied problems. Meet friends and make visits. It may help you to be better organized.]

I don't care what you say, 18,000 pounds (sterling) is a lot of money. The British Government had instructed me to pay it to the man at the corner table who was now using knife and fork to commit ritual murder on a cream pastry.

This is from *The Ipcress File*, Len Deighton's first spy thriller featuring Harry Palmer, the name given to the narrator in his screen incarnation. Deighton does several things here to involve the reader. First, he uses the horoscope to strike a familiar chord. Harry is a spy but the horoscope sets him up as an ordinary bloke, too, someone who starts the day by reading his stars. Subsequent chapters begin in the same way. Whether we believe in horoscopes or not, most of us can't resist reading one when it's in front of us. When Harry does the same, we recognise our own world in his.

Next he puts Harry in a scene. Scenes are visual. We imagine ourselves looking around, just as the character does. Finally, Deighton has Harry speak in first-person viewpoint. This is an intimate style of writing, which brings the character closer to the reader. Even the words Harry uses: 'I don't care what you say . . .' suggests that he's talking directly to us. Deighton has pointed out that when he started the book he did it 'as though I were writing a letter to an old, intimate and trusted friend'.

Deighton's combination of ingredients constructs a bridge between Harry's world and the readers. When readers recognise aspects of their own world in that of the character, the story has relevance to them and their lives. It's a bit like the time we saw the Queen's Tupperware laid out on her breakfast table. It brought her closer to us because it's so normal.

The escapist element of popular fiction derives from this combination of ordinary and extraordinary, familiar with unfamiliar. It's a relaxing form of literature because, once we cross the bridge, we are into a world where we can enjoy identifying with an idealised self-image. Kingsley Amis, who was a big fan of James Bond stories, once remarked that we don't want to have dinner with Bond, or play golf with him. We want to *be* Bond.

While that may not be true for everyone, it's certainly the case that Ian Fleming, Bond's creator, was a master at constructing scenes that bridged the gap between character and readers. Take, for example, the opening to *The Man with the Golden Gun*, in which Bond reappears in London, having been missing for a year. He telephones his department and asks to speak to M or Miss Moneypenny. After an unhelpful circuit of switchboard operators, he is finally through to Captain Walker, a Liaison Officer who pretends he's never heard of M, and is Bond sure he has the right number? Bond patiently gives the number of the Secret Service outside line:

> *'Yes,' said Captain Walker sympathetically. 'We seem to have got that part of it right. But I'm afraid I can't place these people you want to talk to. Who exactly are they? This Mr Em, for instance, I don't think we've got anyone of that name at the Ministry.'*

At this point, I could not stop myself feeling frustrated – which was odd because Bond himself displayed no such emotion. What I had done was to step into Bond's shoes and imagine myself in that situation. Obstructive officialdom is something with which we all have to deal, whether it's one of the utility companies, the

local council or even our broadband provider. Only last week...
no, no, no, I won't even go there. Suffice to say that when
recognition of something in the story world tips over into
empathy with a character, we're already hooked.

In the above example, Fleming uses an emotionally tinged
situation to create empathy. But we are physical creatures, too,
something that's always worth keeping in mind. Lee Child's fast-
moving thrillers often begin with a touch of physical discomfort –
something else to which everyone can relate. Here's the first
paragraph of *Killing Floor,* in which Child introduces us to Jack
Reacher:

> *I was arrested in Eno's diner. At twelve o'clock. I was eating*
> *eggs and drinking coffee. A late breakfast, not lunch. I was*
> *wet and tired after a long walk in heavy rain. All the way*
> *from the highway to the edge of town.*

The food and the feeling of being wet and tired are things we all
recognise. Similarly, although we may never have been arrested
ourselves, it doesn't look like a fun end to a difficult morning. We
don't yet know who Reacher is but we feel stirrings of empathy
with a man who's carted off in the middle of breakfast. We're on
our way across the bridge and into the narrative.

At the start of a story, all these ingredients will help you to get
the reader on your side – or rather the character's side. They're
not just for thrillers:

> *OK, don't panic. Don't panic. It's only a Visa bill. It's a*
> *piece of paper; a few numbers. I mean, just how scary can a*
> *few numbers be?*

That's the first paragraph of Sophie Kinsella's *Diary of a Shopaholic*. Here we have first-person viewpoint, an emotionally charged scene, containing something we all recognise: the credit card bill. Same ingredients – very different story. Have a go yourself. Try out the options in the following exercise.

THE EXERCISE

◆ To give you practice in writing character-bonding opening scenes, do a creative search, using either 'everyday frustrations' or 'physical discomfort' as a trigger.

◆ When you've finished your search, choose one idea and write a short scene, using first-person viewpoint.

◆ If you prefer something a little less structured, write a character's horoscope for the day (See the *Ipcress File* example) and then freewrite a scene using the horoscope to start.

27

Start Your Novel Today

Would you love to write a novel but simply can't get started?
Perhaps you don't have the time or perhaps it just seems like too
big a mountain to climb? All that planning, all those words, it's
enough to make you faint – or at least scuttle sideways, muttering
'Maybe tomorrow.'

Trust me, there's hope. While it's true that novels do contain
rather a lot of words, chapters can be as short as you like:

> *Someone once told me that, in France alone, a quarter of a*
> *million letters are delivered every year to the dead. What she*
> *didn't tell me is that sometimes the dead write back.*

That's the first chapter – yes, the entire chapter – of Joanne
Harris's *Peaches for Monsieur le Curé*. William Faulkner's *As I
Lay Dying* contains one that's only five words: *My mother is a
fish*. Lawrence Block beats both in *Chip Harrison Scores Again*
with '*CHIP, I'M PREGNANT.*' That takes care of the time issue.
Even the busiest among you can find time for a few words a day.
But what about the plotting? And the subplotting and – no, no,
no, it's just too fiddly.

Again, while it's true that many – perhaps most – mass-market
novels do contain carefully structured plots, it isn't written in
stone that this is the only way to write. Alexander McCall Smith

has a different approach in his *44 Scotland Street* series of books, which started life as a daily serial in *The Scotsman* newspaper. Instead of completing the whole thing in advance, McCall Smith wrote each day's segment just ahead of publication. Was it onerous? Quite the contrary. He enjoyed the writing so much that he could not bear to say goodbye to the characters when the first serial ended, so he carried on.

And the plotting? McCall Smith says he's more interested in what makes characters tick. 'I alighted upon a formula that seemed to me to be a good vehicle for a story of this nature. Invent a house containing a number of flats, people it with a good mixture of characters, and then let them get on with it. Any author of fiction will tell you that characters don't need to be told what to do.'

It's a formula that seems to work. Readers liked the bite-sized segments, the quirky characters, and the rambling gossipy story of everyday life. The serial ran for over five years, resulting in the publication of six books in the series. When McCall Smith eventually took a break, he found that he missed the challenge of writing the short segments. He started a new serial, *Corduroy Mansions*. First published online on the *Daily Telegraph* website, that, too, became a book series.

So what exactly is involved? In both series, the thread that connects the characters is the building in which they live. *44 Scotland Street* is in the Bohemian part of Edinburgh's New Town. *Corduroy Mansions* is a large, shabby mansion block in Pimlico, London. Although the actual buildings are fictitious, the neighbourhoods are real, which gives each book a pleasant air of authenticity. If you want to follow McCall Smith's example, try setting your building in your own town, village or country environment and let the characters patronise the local shops, pubs and cafes.

When it comes to the cast of characters, a 'good mix' will include people who are different from each other in personality, attitudes and ages. For example, in *44 Scotland Street*, we have a student on her second gap year, renting a room from a young, narcissistic chartered surveyor, a pushy mother with her precocious six-year-old son, and a middle-aged widow who is also an anthropologist and drives a custard-coloured Mercedes-Benz 560. *Corduroy Mansions* starts out with an equally eccentric blend of 12 main characters. We'll look at just one: William French, a widowed wine merchant, who occupies the top-floor flat with his 23-year-old son, Eddie and a small dog called Freddie de la Hay, who is a character in his own right.

McCall Smith introduces us to William in the first segment, entitled 'In the Bathroom'. It's an introspective little scene in which William looks into his bathroom mirror, worrying about getting older and the pros and cons of cosmetic surgery. Having decided that he'd prefer to age naturally in a National Trust sort of way, he wonders how he'd describe himself in a lonely hearts ad. *Solvent* and *shortly to be in reasonable shape* seem accurate, but what about his own requirements? Here's a taster:

> *Now, what about: would like to meet presentable, lively*
> *woman. Well, presentable was a pretty low requirement.*
> *Virtually anybody could be presentable if they made at least*
> *some effort. Lively was another matter. One would have to be*
> *careful about lively because it could possibly be code for*
> *insatiable, and that would not do. Who would want to meet an*
> *insatiable woman? My son, thought William suddenly. That's*

*exactly the sort of woman Eddie would want to meet. The
thought depressed him.*

As you can see, McCall Smith uses William's introspection to
reveal aspects of his character, his preoccupations and his
relationship with his son. It's idiosyncratic, it's gentle and it has
that wonderful edge of humour that has helped to make McCall
Smith one of the world's favourite writers. Now, in plot-driven
fiction, a morning bathroom scene might lack the dynamic action
needed to jump-start the story. In character-driven fiction, that's
not so much of a problem and bathroom scenes can be useful for
several reasons:

1. Bathroom accoutrements give a character something to do
    during the introspection, so there's an illusion of activity. As
    thoughts flow, s/he can get on with running a bath, cleaning
    teeth and so on.

2. The mirror allows characters to look at themselves and make
    comments about appearance without artifice. We all look at
    ourselves in bathroom mirrors, so we accept that characters do
    the same.

3. Bathrooms encourage reflection, so it seems natural for a
    character to engage in interior monologue. And because a
    bathroom is a private place, the monologue gains authenticity.
    The character is stripped bare on a psychological level.

But where, you might be wondering, does McCall Smith find his
characters? In the preface to *44 Scotland Street* he reveals that
they all reflect human types he has encountered in his own life.
And there's more good news. When asked in a television interview
how he develops the characters, he replied that he doesn't tend to

develop them in advance. Instead, they 'walk onto the page' as he's writing. One of the readers' favourite *Scotland Street* characters, six-year-old Bertie, whose mother forces him to learn Italian and play the saxophone, appeared from 'nowhere'.

Have I whetted your appetite? Try the following exercise.

THE EXERCISE

Choose a character – any character – and write your own bathroom scene. If you can't think of a character, choose a name and go from there. Let the character come to you.

Note: When *Corduroy Mansions* first appeared in its digital format, McCall Smith provided brief – around 50 words – Personal Information pieces for each character, including age, profession, significant relationships, likes, and dislikes. These were designed to give readers an opportunity to submit their own scenes for possible inclusion in the novel. You can still find these personal pieces on the *Telegraph* website. Just enter 'Corduroy Mansions personal information' into Google.

28

Catch Me If You Can

Whenever I ask writing class members what they like in an exercise, I get a variety of different answers. Most people want something useful and easy to do, but what they really love is having a bit of fun. The next exercise wins on all three counts. The idea for it came to me after watching *The Bourne Ultimatum* on television. If you've seen this film, you may remember the extra-long chase sequence near the end, in which Jason Bourne tries to catch up with an assassin before he reaches his target. Bourne himself is being chased by the local police, who think he's responsible for an earlier explosion. It's an exciting sequence with lots of rushing in and out of buildings, jumping from roof to roof, plus dead ends, locked doors, and walls topped by broken glass – a bit like a thriller version of *Monopoly*.

What is it about chase sequences that makes them so compelling? They appear in so many different types of story, but essentially they are all the same whether they take place on rooftops, in cars, on horseback, or in the sewers, as in Victor Hugo's *Les Misérables*. Someone does the running, while someone else chases. It's cat and mouse, hunter and hunted, hide-and-seek. Sometimes, the story itself is one long chase – think of John Buchan's *The Thirty-Nine Steps*, in which Richard Hannay is a man on the run from both the police and German spies. And that gives us a clue to the chase's enduring popularity. The chase is not just a sequence. It's a basic plot in its own right. Let's unpick this a little.

A basic plot is one that contains archetypes. An archetype is a recurring model or pattern of behaviour that we all recognise. In *Narratives of Human Evolution* Misia Landau suggests that these recurring basic patterns are a kind of universal psychic grammar. We all understand them because they have meaning for us on an anthropological level. If we apply this to 'the chase', it's certainly true that even very young children understand the concept. You have only to say 'Coming to catch you!' to hear them squeal with delight. Later, of course, they like chasing things themselves, such as pigeons in the park or other children in the playground.

In other words, the chase dynamic is hardwired in our brains. Why? An evolutionary explanation might be that our Palaeolithic ancestors' survival depended on it. They had to chase their food. They also had to be prepared to run if the food turned belligerent and started chasing them. Times have changed, but our fight-or-flight mechanism remains an automatic reflex. When that reflex kicks in, our heart rate increases, our adrenaline surges and our senses are heightened – the same physical sensations we experience during a chase narrative on film or in print. The chase may be fiction but our excitement is real.

When writers use chase sequences or chase plots they tap into these archetypal patterns, which in turn trigger the readers' emotional response. Although the basic elements stay the same, however, we still have to give the plot a fresh set of 'clothes' every time we use it. As Ronald B. Tobias points out in his excellent *20 Master Plots (and How to Build Them)*: 'If you resort to standard clichés, the chase won't have the excitement your reader demands. If the territory is too familiar, you'll have a harder time getting the reader involved. Your key to keeping the chase exciting is to make it unpredictable.'

And how do we do that? We practise our skills in divergent – or creative – thinking. I talked about divergent thinking in my last book, *The Five-Minute Writer,* but just to refresh your memory, divergent thinking is a combination of fluency (thinking of lots of ideas), flexibility (thinking outside the box, from different angles) and originality (thinking of ideas that are statistically unusual). Not only will practice in divergent thinking help you to develop twists and turns in a chase story, but it will also help you with plotting in general. Run for your life with the following exercise.

THE EXERCISE

1. Think of a place you know with lots of different roads or streets. It could be part of a city, or a small town or village. It could even be a place in your imagination. In writing classes, I usually hand out photocopies of an A5-sized tourist map of Bath because it identifies lots of different landmarks we can use in the exercise.

2. Got your map? Good. Now for the fun bit. At one end of the map, you have a character who wants to reach an address at the other end. The character is in a hurry, having given their pursuer the slip. On the Bath map, we start the character off at the Holburne Museum. The goal is to reach the Royal Crescent at the other end of town.

3. Your task is to make it as difficult as possible for the character to reach their destination. So, short of killing them, think of as many obstacles/diversions/blind alleys as you can. Feel free to come up with silly ideas. What if a jackdaw steals the character's glasses so they can't see where they're going? That's fine. What you can't do is to have the glasses miraculously appear again. Having introduced an obstacle, the character has to find a way to deal with it and carry on before the pursuer catches up with them. Remember, too, that your character may be able to move below ground and above it as well as on it.

When you've finished, read on.

What you've done, whether it felt like it or not, is to write a simple plot.

1. Plot is a sequence of events with the emphasis on causality.

2. Plot involves some kind of goal towards which the characters struggle, encountering obstacles and opposition.

A published novel or story may be nowhere near as simple as being chased across town, but if you apply the kind of thinking you used for this exercise, you will end up with a plotted piece of fiction.

29

Snippet Trigger – Trapped

What is your opinion of flat-pack furniture? Love it or hate it, we've probably all bought an item at some time in our lives, only to rue the day when we try to decipher the nonsense instructions, translated by someone whose knowledge of languages is as shaky as the assembled product with half the screws missing – as of course they often are. But I bet – and I admit I'm just guessing here – that you've never managed to assemble a piece of furniture with yourself inside it? Well, count yourself lucky. A snippet in the national dailies reports that a woman in Leicestershire dialled 999 after getting stuck for 90 minutes inside a flat-pack wardrobe she was trying to put together. According to Leicestershire Fire and Rescue Service: 'She wasn't that unhappy as she had her cigarettes with her while she was waiting to be rescued.' The incident made it onto the Service's list of 'unusual' calls.

This is the kind of wacky story I love to cut out and paste in my ideas book. Its central theme of being trapped and then freed is an excellent example of Claude Levi-Strauss's theory of binary opposition, which states that our brains find meaning in abstract concepts by automatically contrasting them with their opposites. 'Darkness' for example, takes on meaning only when contrasted with 'light'. Great stories often go for the big ones, like good and evil or love and hate, because these generate powerfully emotive plotlines, but all successful fiction contains oppositions in some form or other.

Why use oppositions? Without them, a story is bland – like a white sheet of paper with nothing to relieve it. Add a black stripe and you have modern art. Ian Falconer's *Olivia's Opposites* even uses simple illustrations of 'up' and 'down', 'open' and 'closed' to introduce the basics to toddlers.

As a theme, 'trapped' is versatile. We're familiar with the '24-hours-before-the-oxygen-runs-out' variety, but we can use it in many different kinds of fiction. Classic examples include *The Man in the Iron Mask* by Alexandre Dumas, *The Prisoner of Zenda* by Anthony Hope Hawkins, and the fairytale *Rapunzel,* in which a young girl is trapped in a tower with no door or staircase. It makes for a strong storyline because its goal – escape or freedom – is a constant presence even when it isn't explicit. This makes it ideal for both mass-market and literary fiction, where the meaning of trapped is often more psychological than literal. In James Joyce's *Dubliners* short story collection, for example, there are no daring escape scenes from burning buildings, underground tunnels – or even wardrobes. Instead, many of the characters feel trapped by circumstances – by poverty, loneliness, or family pressures. We'll look at just one.

In *A Little Cloud*, Little Chandler is a married man with a small baby. The story begins when Chandler meets an old friend, Gallaher, in the pub. Gallaher, now a successful journalist, is a single man and boasts of his travels to London and Paris. This ignites feelings of lost ambition in Little Chandler. He arrives home, having forgotten to collect a packet of Bewley's coffee for his wife, Annie. She is *short* with him and goes out to buy the coffee herself, leaving him to mind the baby. Chandler starts to brood. He looks at a framed photo of Annie with her pretty face and calm eyes, and finds her composure irritating. Why, he asks himself, had he married the eyes in the photograph?

> *He caught himself up in the question and glanced nervously round the room. He found something mean in the pretty furniture which he had bought for his house on the hire system. Annie had chosen it herself and it reminded him of her. It too was prim and pretty. A dull resentment against his life awoke within him. Could he not escape from his little house? Was it too late for him to try to live bravely like Gallaher? Could he go to London? There was the furniture still to be paid for. If he could only write a book and get it published, that might open the way for him.*

Feeling thoroughly disgruntled, Little Chandler picks up a volume of Byron's poems and wonders if he could write like that. When the baby begins to cry, however, his fantasies come to an abrupt end and real life once more asserts itself. But is Little Chandler really trapped? In the sense that we are all constrained by the choices we make in life, yes. However, the title of the story, *A Little Cloud,* suggests that tomorrow, with Gallaher gone, little Chandler will not be too unhappy with his lot. Like most of the stories in *Dubliners, A Little Cloud* articulates how a character's perception of reality colours his experience of it.

For any writer in search of a plot or just an inspirational trigger, 'trapped' is rich compost into which we can delve for lots of different ideas. Try the following exercise.

THE EXERCISE

◆ Do a creative search, using the word 'trapped' as a trigger. Include as many different examples, both literal and metaphorical, as you can, including the titles of any films or books that come to mind.

◆ To boost your ideas still further, think about the different genres. How would 'trapped' work in romance, in sci-fi, crime or fantasy? Remember, too, that children's books can often be a great source of inspiration. I remember a young adult suspense novel that combined almost all the genres. In Lois Duncan's *Locked in Time,* a mother finds a potion which stops her children growing up. They are trapped in time, until the mother remarries and her new stepdaughter suspects something strange.

◆ When you have a few ideas to hand, choose one to explore in more detail, either as a freewrite or, if you prefer to plan, a rough outline detailing the main characters and how the story might develop.

$$\left(30\right)$$

The Answer to Life, the Universe
. . . and What to Write Next

'All right,' said Deep Thought. 'The Answer to the Great Question . . .'

'Yes . . . !'

'Of Life, the Universe and Everything . . .' said Deep Thought.

'Yes . . . !'

'Is . . .' said Deep Thought, and paused.

'Yes . . . !'

'Is . . .'

'Yes . . . !!! . . . ?'

'Forty-two,' said Deep Thought, with infinite majesty and calm.

Douglas Adams, The Hitchhiker's Guide to the Galaxy

If you've ever read, listened to or watched *The Hitchhiker's Guide,* you will remember that Deep Thought, the supercomputer specially built to answer the Great Question, took seven and a half million years before coming up with this infuriatingly obscure answer. When challenged, the computer answers loftily that the real problem is that the questioners have never actually known what the question is. Once they know that, they'll be better placed to understand why 42 is the right answer.

It's a wonderfully quirky and funny scene, unless of course you've recently had to communicate with a real supercomputer, in which case, keep trying, you're next in the queue. But there's always a bright side. While you're waiting, try the following exercise. It will use up five minutes, it's as easy as pie, and you'll have a piece of writing to show at the end.

THE EXERCISE

Pick a novel – any novel – and turn to page 42. Find the first complete sentence at the top of the page. That's your trigger. Copy the sentence down and just start writing. Ignore the original story. This is your piece now. If there's no bookshelf or ebook reader handy, feel free to use one of these sentences instead. All of them come from page 42.

But there was nothing. (Peter James, *Sweet Heart*)

Mrs Forbes at school said that when Mother died she had gone to Heaven. (Mark Haddon, *The Curious Incident of the Dog in the Night-Time*)

Her hand brushed mine like a cool breath. (Joanne Harris, *Chocolat*)

He never mentioned a word about this to her or let her know that he had been snooping into her life. (Stieg Larsson, *The Girl with the Dragon Tattoo*)

31

A Bunch of Parsley and a Baked Alaska

I once met a cookery writer who said that when she found a recipe she wanted to pass off as her own, she just added a bunch of parsley to the list of ingredients. As she pointed out, there are only so many basic recipes and everything else is just a variation.

I was a little shocked, until I remembered that fiction writers have always done much the same thing when creating characters. In fact, some pulp writers don't even bother adding the parsley, which is why their stories are populated by stereotypes. We all know these characters: the absent-minded professor, the tough-talking cop, the romantic heroine who only needs to brush her (always glossy) hair and put on designer clothes to look gorgeous, even first thing in the morning.

'Say no to stereotypes' is standard advice, but before we throw them all out with their bathwater, let's take a closer look. In real life, stereotyping involves making assumptions about an individual based on their association with a specific group whose defining qualities we already know – or think we do. This is often castigated as prejudice, but the cognitive process underpinning it is categorisation, without which we could not function. When we see a dog, for example, we don't evaluate it from scratch. Instead, our brain matches it against the category 'dogs' already stored in our memory, including everything we know about dogs from previous encounters with them.

When we meet people, the same process automatically clicks into action. We see, we hear, we categorise. Oh, we say, s/he's the arty type, a yummy mummy, French, and so on. As Theodore Goodman writes in *The Writing of Fiction:* 'The type is enormously economical in enabling us to respond at a stroke to great numbers of individuals... Types are like branches, any branches, which our simian hands seize, and on which we swing through the dense social woods.' Indeed, judging by the proliferation of all those multiple-choice 'personality' quizzes, most of us can't resist slotting ourselves into the latest cultural categories. I even found one on the Internet which sorts people into different types of cheese. In case you're interested, I'm blue cheese. Go figure – as an American friend used to say.

In fiction, types and stereotypes are shorthand representations of characters we recognise, either from real life or from previous encounters in a particular genre. The line between type and stereotype is blurred and really depends on how each is used. While type characters are often defined by a single dominant trait, a stereotype usually comes with its own implicit narrative. The laconic private eye who likes a drink and talks tough, for example, is a classic stereotype whereas the 'gossip' could be any number of different characters.

Using character types has a long and distinguished history. Henry Fielding used them, so did Dickens. However, one of the first writers to compile a comprehensive list was Aristotle's student, the Greek philosopher Theophrastus, whose *Characters* is a collection of short sketches describing 30 types of individuals encountered in the streets of fourth-century BC Athens. They have time-travelled well. Take The Garrulous Man:

The Garrulous Man is one who will sit down beside a person whom he does not know, and first pronounce a panegyric on his own wife; then relate his dream of last night; then go through in detail what he has had for dinner. Then, warming to the work, he will remark that the men of the present day are greatly inferior to the ancients; and how cheap wheat has become in the market; and what a number of foreigners are in town; and that the sea is navigable after the Dionysia; and that, if Zeus would send more rain, the crops would be better; and that he will work his land next year; and how hard it is to live.

When I read this character sketch, I could not help smiling because I know quite a few people who fit this description, including a member of my family. I bet you do, too. Most of the other character types – The Grumbler, The Flatterer, The Evil-speaker – are equally recognisable and could be plucked straight from Athens into your local pub. Such type characters appeal to the reader at first meeting because they are familiar, a bit like old friends with whom we feel comfortable.

If, however, the writer makes no attempt to freshen them up, the familiar feeling will quickly turn to boredom. This is where that bunch of parsley comes in handy, or as J. G. Cawelti calls it in *Adventure, Mystery, and Romance: Formula Stories as Art and Popular Culture,* 'stereotype vitalization'. Cawelti points to two particularly effective ways to achieve this. The first, which is more Baked Alaska than parsley, is to blend two very different stereotypes together. Cawelti cites Sherlock Holmes, the stereotypical 'rational, scientific investigator'. However, his character 'incorporates basic qualities from a contrary stereotype, that of the dreamy romantic poet, for Holmes is also a man of intuition, a dreamer and a drug taker, who spends hours fiddling aimlessly on his violin'. Taken individually, each of these stereotypes is stale. When combined, the result is a character of striking idiosyncrasy.

The second technique is one advocated by Aristotle. You start with a basic type and then add additional particularising features: weaknesses, flaws, unexpected facets to make the character more complex and less predictable. In the television series *Doc Martin*, for example, the doctor has a problem with blood – he faints at the sight of it. We don't expect that. Similarly, in the Scandinavian crime serial *The Bridge*, first broadcast on BBC4, Saga Norén has all the brilliant powers of deduction and workaholic attitude we've come to expect of fictional detectives. But instead of the usual male loner with attitude, Saga is a woman with ice queen looks and Asperger Syndrome traits. As a result, she is one of the freshest detectives we've seen in a long while, the perfect example of vitalisation.

Armed with these two techniques, you can create characters the readers will adore. The following exercise will give you ideas.

THE EXERCISE

◆ Start compiling your own 'Theophrastus' collection of character types. These might be people you know (the office bore, the possessive spouse, the fair-weather friend), people you've observed in everyday life, or even fictional characters. Remember that while basic personality types (introvert, extravert) stay the same, other types, such as the Yuppie and the WAG come and go, according to what is going on in our culture.

◆ Choose a character type and add particularising details to create a fresh character. Remember that what you're trying to achieve is a character with some unexpected traits, interests or flaws. A rural vicar who likes rock music will hold the reader's interest longer than one who grows roses. A psychopath who collects dolls is more intriguing – and chilling – than one who sits at home looking at porn. If you need help choosing a type, here are some options.

The Grumbler	The Enthusiast	The Liar
The Meanie	The Smartphone Addict	The Perfectionist
The Boaster	The Romantic Dreamer	The Procrastinator
The Loner	The Control Freak	The Do-gooder

◆ Once you have your vitalised type, write a short scene in which the character reveals himself/herself.

32

Alphabet Triggers

Don't you love those serendipitous moments when you discover something interesting while looking for something completely different? The following exercise came out of the blue while I was trying to trace a poem by Robert Browning before my Monday evening writing class. I found it on the BBC's Poetry Season website, but it was the site's 'Search poems by theme' facility that captured my attention. Arranged alphabetically and in different-sized fonts, the list is almost a poem in its own right:

ageing animals art beauty
celebration childhood conflict desire
faith *family* fantasy farewells ...

And so it continues to the end of the alphabet – almost. There were no items beginning with 'Z'. What struck me about the list was its emotive quality, the richness of its themes, all of which had no doubt been picked out by computer on the basis of frequency. What we have here is not just the stuff of great poetry, but of life itself, which makes it ideal for prose writers, too. I had a light bulb moment, scribbled down the list and rushed off to class, armed with a new five-minute exercise. Try it now yourself. It worked well in our session.

◆ Starting with the letter 'A', jot down the first few words or themes that float into your head. Note that the Poetry Season list contains mainly abstract words – that is things that we experience in thought or ideas but not necessarily in concrete form. For fiction writers, such abstract words – ageing, for example – are likely to be more inspirational than concrete words like apple. If you're an article writer, a mix of concrete and abstract themes will work well. Move on to 'B' and do the same, and so on through the alphabet. It's not a race against time. When your five minutes is up, stop – at whatever letter you have reached. You can always continue another day.

◆ Look at your list. What you now have is a set of triggers that have meaning for you, if not on a conscious level, then a subconscious one. Choose one word for a five-minute freewrite or – if you're into poetry – a short poem. Alternatively, just pick a word from the BBC Poetry Season's list. (You may still find the complete list on the web if you put 'BBC Poetry Season' into your search engine.)

Note: When we did this exercise in class, one student's first word was 'Ardvaark'. He was delighted to have an opportunity of using it, not because of his enthusiasm for nocturnal mammals of South Africa, but because he's a bit of a logophile. As a retired English teacher, he loves words. That's fine. However, the list is not really about knowledge. Rather, it's about inspiration and you may find that simple emotive words work better in your freewrite.

33

Survival Strategies

In 2010, an incredible story of survival rocked the world. The San José mine in northern Chile collapsed and 33 miners were buried alive. After two months underground, they were brought to the surface in a tiny 'Phoenix' capsule barely wider than a man's shoulders. It took 15 minutes for each to make the half-mile journey, alone, in the dark, and with the knowledge that the capsule might get stuck on the way. For 22 hours, anyone with a television was able to see the rescue happening in real time. When the final miner emerged into fresh air, the watching world breathed a collective sigh of relief.

Survival against the odds touches a universal chord. We imagine ourselves in a similar situation and wonder how we'd cope. As a lifelong claustrophobic who gets jumpy when elevator doors take a long time to open, I found the miners' story the stuff of nightmares, but I was still gripped. In the real world, survival is our most fundamental need. Consequently, in fiction, a story about characters fighting for their lives will always resonate. It might be an end-of-the-world-as-we-know-it plot like Stephen King's *The Stand,* a sci-fi classic like John Wyndham's *The Day of the Triffids*, in which humans are at the mercy of homicidal plants, or Jack London's *The Call of the Wild*, in which the main character is a dog kidnapped from his home, beaten with clubs, and then shipped to the frozen wastes of Alaska to pull sledges during the Klondike gold rush.

Such stories give us the vicarious opportunity to engage with life-threatening challenges and become heroic. Great adversity brings out the best – and sometimes the worst – in us, but that's part of the deal. There is nothing subtle about the conflict in survival plots. It's a stark choice. Take action or die. As a result, a new breed of survival fiction has recently become popular with young adults, whose time might otherwise be spent in playing computer games. The phenomenal success of Suzanne Collins's *The Hunger Games* trilogy, later made into an equally successful film, is a case in point. When the first book appeared, it didn't appeal to me. Then, during a cut and blow-dry, my hairdresser – whose reading tastes are eclectic – asked me if I'd read it. At first, he was apologetic. 'It's really a teen novel,' he said, 'but it's so exciting, I'm almost afraid to turn the page.' Enough said. I bought the book.

The Hunger Games is a futuristic novel set in the fictional dystopia of Panem. Like other dystopias – Orwell's *Nineteen Eighty-Four* is a classic example – it features standard ingredients: food shortages, no-entry zones, and the suppression of its people by a brutal state. Its main motif, however, is a reworking of the Greek legend of Theseus and the Minotaur. Every year, a lottery selects 24 teenagers, who are then forced to fight each other to the death on a live TV show. There is only one winner. Against this nightmarish backdrop, the viewpoint character, Katniss Everdeen, is shocked to hear that her little sister's name has been selected:

> *Somewhere far away, I can hear the crowd murmuring unhappily, as they always do when a twelve-year-old gets chosen, because no one thinks this is fair. And then I see her, the blood drained from her face, hands clenched in fists at her sides, walking with stiff, small steps up towards the stage,*

*passing me, and I see the back of her blouse has become
untucked and hangs out over her skirt. It's this detail, the
untucked blouse forming a duck's tail, that brings me back to
myself.*

Katniss volunteers to take her sister's place. For anyone else, it
might be a death sentence, but Katniss is not your average 16-
year-old. She's a skilled archer, using her bow and arrows to hunt
for food, and selling the surplus on the black market. For Katniss,
survival is second nature.

It's a long way from *The Wizard of Oz,* but *The Hunger Games* is
not just an exercise in nihilism. It has positive messages, too, one
being that exposure to stressful life events does not have to
destroy you. There is brutality and injustice in the real world, but
it is our reaction to such things that makes us what we are.
Grimm's fairy tales have been standard children's literature for
generations, yet many of the stories contain horrifying scenes. In
Hansel and Gretel, for example, the wicked witch fattens up
Hansel for the oven, while his sister Gretel has to light the fire. It
is Gretel's quick thinking that saves both their lives. When the
witch tells her to get into the oven to check that it's hot enough,
Gretal gives her a push and closes the oven door: *Eek! How
horribly she screamed. But Gretel ran away and the wicked witch
burned miserably to death.*

According to Anna North, whose novel *America Pacifica* is a
dystopian story of survival in a second ice age, the appeal of such
fiction for young people is its focus on coming of age:
'Adolescence is a time when your character is still being formed,
and it's exciting to read about young people who, by facing really
extreme hardships, are formed into something great.'

In one sense, of course, we are all survivors. To be alive is to have survived – that's the law of evolutionary psychology. But in the modern Western world, where we no longer have to hunt for our food, the focus has shifted from physical to psychological survival. We all need strategies for that and we start to develop them early. For example, a young child who has scribbled all over the sitting room in red crayon may simply deny it when challenged. Similarly, in adulthood, we may use denial to protect ourselves from uncomfortable truths or difficult situations. In Lolly Winston's *Sophie's Bakery for the Broken Hearted*, Sophie Stanton is in denial after losing her husband at an early age:

> *How can I be a widow? Widows wear horn-rimmed glasses and cardigan sweaters that smell like mothballs and have crepe paper skin and names like Gladys and Midge and meet with their other widow friends once a week to play pinochle. I'm only thirty-six.*

At first, Sophie can't cope. She does crazy things, like going to work in her bathrobe and driving her car through a garage door, before she finally works through her grief and rebuilds her life. She survives. Fiction thrives on such characters: men, women, children and even animals whose lives are blown off course by a traumatic event. In the real world, we face these situations at every stage of our lives. For example, can you remember your first day at school? I can. My biscuits went missing. I was distraught.

According to Joanna Trollope, whose emotionally charged novels tackle contemporary themes – broken homes, adoption, adultery – the worse a situation is in real life, the better it is for fiction. Her characters often behave badly and hurt those close to them. But: 'They haven't devised this way of behaving because they are beastly people, they have devised it to survive.'

◆ Make a list or a creative search of the traumas and scars of your life, starting with childhood and moving up to your present self. In this context, trauma is an emotional response to any event that shocks us psychologically. We all have emotional scars. Like the physical scars of the warrior, they are testament to our survival. Readers love characters who've been through the mill, yet lived to tell the tale. When you've finished your search, choose one particular experience or scar to explore in more detail.

◆ Imagine you have been washed up on a fantasy island. All you have with you are your wits. How will you survive? Enjoy your fantasy.

◆ Write about a character who is having a survival problem in one of the following areas of their life; choose one to explore in a short story:

Holidays	Work	Relationships
Christmas/other celebrations	Moving home	Children

$$\left(34\right)$$

Log Lines

In writing classes, I sometimes suggest that would-be novelists construct log lines. A log line is a dynamic one- or two-sentence summary of a story, designed to arouse interest. Distilling the essence of your story into so few words is a challenge but scriptwriters do it all the time. Studio executives and producers receive thousands of scripts a year. An intriguing log line tells them which ones deserve a closer look. Similarly, in television listings, log lines allow viewers to decide if a film is worth watching. Here are a couple you might recognise:

> *In the bleak days of the Cold War, espionage veteran George Smiley is forced from semi-retirement to uncover a Soviet agent within MI6's echelons.*
> (John Le Carré, *Tinker Tailor Soldier Spy*)

> *In a parallel universe, young Lyra Belacqua journeys to the far North to save her best friend and other kidnapped children from terrible experiments by a mysterious organisation.*
> (Philip Pullman, *The Golden Compass*)

Why bother with log lines if you're not a scriptwriter? First, if you've already written your novel, the process of constructing a log line can alert you to essential plotting elements that might be missing. We'll look at what those are in a moment. Second, log lines allow you to test story ideas before you start writing. Finally, log lines help you to clarify your thoughts when you're trying to sell. Writers' conferences are great places to pitch your work to agents and publishers, but time is tight and it's easy to become flustered. A clear and concise summary will immediately send the signal that you know what you're doing. You can always expand when the agent shows interest – and they are more likely to do this if your story sounds intriguing.

OK, let's get down to business. The best log lines contain the following essential ingredients: a goal, a character's incentive for pursuing that goal, and conflict. To weave these elements into a tempting log line, ask yourself four questions:

1. Who is the story about? (Main character or characters)

2. What kickstarts the story into action? (Incentive)

3. What does the character want to achieve? (Goal)

4. Who or what stands in the way? (Conflict)

For example, take another look at the log line for *The Golden Compass*. Does it answer the above questions? Yes, it does – in a neatly crafted nutshell. The main character is Lyra Belacqua. The incident that kickstarts the story into action is the kidnapping of Lyra's best friend. Lyra's goal is to rescue her friend and other kidnapped children. The conflict comes from the mysterious organisation performing the experiments. Note that the log line doesn't explain what the organisation is or that its experiments involve severing the children's daemons. Instead, it uses non-specific adjectives – 'terrible' and 'mysterious' – which provoke questions without giving too much away.

On the other hand, giving too little away or trying to manage without one of the essential ingredients is a recipe for dullness.

For example, how would you rate this one for *How to Steal a Million,* starring Audrey Hepburn: A woman hires a detective to steal a forged sculpture.

Not exactly sparkling, is it? That's partly because the log line gives no indication of what kind of story this is, but mainly because the woman's incentive for stealing the sculpture – the element that kickstarts the action – is missing. Let's try again:

> *Romantic comedy about a woman who must steal a statue from a Paris museum to help conceal her father's art forgeries, and the man who helps her.*

It's just a few extra words, but those words add emotion and motivation, which makes all the difference to our perception of the story. Here is a woman driven to crime to protect her family. And it's set in Paris. Our interest is piqued.

It's fair to say that some stories are more challenging than others. For example, many novels are written from more than one point of view, with each character having their own personal story. Where does that leave the four essential questions? This is where constructing a log line can really help to clarify the overall structure, because despite the separate characters' stories, there will be – or should be – a main theme or event that connects all the characters and their goals. It might be a war, a natural disaster, or even a setting that acts as a thread. Look for that connective piece of tissue. For example:

> *When a light aircraft comes down in a farmer's field, shocking secrets emerge that threaten the lives of three local families. As they struggle to cope with the truth, a mother and son take*

desperate measures, and a police officer has to choose between love and duty.

I just made that up, but you get the idea? For more examples, check out the Internet Movie Database.

Before you set to work creating log lines for your own stories, try creating one or two for popular novels. You can use any novel, but here are some suggestions to get you started:

Rebecca by Daphne du Maurier

Eragon by Christopher Paolini

The Fellowship of the Ring by J. R. R. Tolkien

Angels and Demons by Dan Brown

Lord of the Flies by William Golding

The Lion, the Witch and the Wardrobe by C. S. Lewis

All these novels have been adapted for the cinema, so feel free to compare the log lines you've written with the official ones on the Internet Movie Database (imdb.com).

35

Put Your Worries on the Page

When you ask professional writers where they get their ideas, the answers are often less than satisfactory, ranging from the vague 'Everywhere' to the facetious 'A small, bloodthirsty elf who lives in a hole under my desk.' Every once in a while, though, someone comes along with a simple technique that everyone can use. Hollywood screenwriter William Martell says that one of his favourite ways to generate ideas is to come up with a character and then figure out what's the worst thing that could happen to that character. Then make it happen.

This is good news for all those of you who worry about things that are (probably) never going to happen. I've spent my whole life doing this, and while the worry might have been justified ten per cent of the time, the other 90 per cent was just a waste of brain activity. But if I hadn't been a worrier, I'd never have been able to write stories about characters getting locked out in their nightwear, breaking their ankles on Christmas Eve, or getting their home-made wine mixed up with weedkiller.

This may not be quite the stuff of Hollywood, but in magazine fiction it works a treat, and once you have your idea you can play around with it. Turn that broken ankle into something more serious, add a beautiful animal, and you have *The Horse Whisperer*. Similarly, a relatively minor worry for an adult may be a big one for a small child or someone with a disability. Take being locked out, for example. I've recently talked to a couple who are looking after an elderly relative with dementia. They've had to put a lock on the kitchen door, because their relative rises in the night and tries to make tea by putting the electric kettle on the gas hob. They worry that she might set the house on fire. It's a situation that could go in many different directions.

This is certainly the stuff of Hollywood and Julie Christie has an Oscar nomination to prove it. In *Away From Her,* Christie plays a woman with Alzheimer's who volunteers to go into a care facility to avoid being a burden on her husband. The film has everything a high-concept movie should have, including conflict, struggle, strong emotion and sacrifice. It started out as *The Bear Came Over the Mountain*, a short story by Alice Munro published in *The New Yorker* magazine.

At the other end of the scale, don't dismiss the small stuff. I know someone who worries so much about going to a new hairdresser that she has to take a beta blocker before her appointment. A bad haircut might not be life-threatening, but our hair is part of our identity and when that identity is threatened, it's not trivial. My hairdresser tells me that when one client was unhappy with her new hair colour she lay down on the floor of the salon and screamed. They took her away in a white van. No, I'm just kidding. But it makes you think. Suppose she were a doctor, a lawyer, or indeed anyone whose effective functioning depends on their composure?

Alternatively, such an incident might inspire a comedy. Worst-case-scenario worries often do. In the Woody Allen film *Hannah and Her Sisters,* for example, Allen's character, Mickey, is a hypochondriac who worries that he has the classic symptoms of a brain tumour. Then someone reminds him that two months ago he thought he had a malignant melanoma on his back, which turned out to be a black spot on his shirt.

Finally, many women worry about losing their wedding rings. That theme might have been overdone, but it can always be given a new twist. In Donald E. Westlake's comedy crime novel *What's the Worst that Could Happen?*, a burglar called Dortmunder has his 'lucky' ring stolen by a rich man whose house he is in the process of robbing. The rest of the book centres on Dortmunder's efforts to retrieve the ring. Hollywood liked that, and made it into a film starring Martin Lawrence and Danny de Vito.

THE EXERCISE

- What do you worry about? Start a worry box. Write down your worries on scraps of paper and drop them into the box. Remember, nothing is too trivial. If you're worried about something, chances are that somebody else shares the same – or similar – worry. Add to the box whenever you like. You will soon have a pile of worries to heap on your characters.

- Create a brief character sketch, including name, age and just a few other details. What does the character worry about? What's the worst thing that could happen to this character? Use it straight or give it a twist, but make it happen.

Repeat as necessary whenever you need a plot.

36

Memories Are Made of This

Have you ever noticed how many songs are associated with place? This is particularly true of blues music, like J. B. Lenoir's *Alabama Blues,* and blues-inspired pieces like Chuck Berry's *Johnny B Goode* about a poor boy near New Orleans. Blues music articulates the early African-American experience and the community's struggle to create a cultural identity after the abolition of slavery. In this struggle, places are imbued with emotional significance. Beale Street in Memphis, for example, now immortalised as the birthplace of rock 'n' roll, became a cultural centre, full of blues and jazz clubs. 'Beale Street was the black man's haven', 'said Rufus Thomas, one of the performers. 'They'd come into town and forget all their worries and woes.'

This connection between place and emotional experience is something we all understand. Place is the backdrop against which we live our lives. As environmental psychologist Maria Giuliani points out, 'Each of us is familiar with the peculiar aspects, nuances of this affective world. It not only permeates our daily life but very often appears in the representations, idealisations and expressions of life and affect represented by art products – in the first instance literature, but also other genres.'

In other words, when writers, including song writers and musicians, use place in their work, those places take on emotional significance for their audiences, too. In the 1960s, teenagers became enthralled with California through songs about San

Francisco and the west coast beaches. We all had a meaningful vision of what it was like, even though most of us had never been there. Fiction plays the same card but without the music. Joyce Carol Oates points to the many novelists who are 'inextricably linked to a region, to a language-dialect of particular sharpness, vividness, and idiosyncrasy'. It is, she says, impossible to read Dickens and not think of Victorian London. Similarly, when we read Daphne du Maurier, most of whose novels are set in Cornwall, the emotive power of her stories is associated with the settings. There are now tourist trails around Fowey, and the various landmarks mentioned in the novels. In France, *Da Vinci Code* fans flock to Paris and particularly the church of St Sulpice, whose authorities have become so irritated by tourists demanding to see where Silas murdered the nun that they have erected notices explaining that the book is fiction.

Place – music – emotion: this is a powerful mix. Lyricists use place to enhance the emotive effect of music. Film-makers use music to enhance the emotive quality of their settings and fiction writers can use music to connect with the past where memories are stored. Any one of these may be just the trigger you need to get you started on a story. Try the following exercise.

THE EXERCISE

Think of the music or songs that have meaning for you: those that are linked to places and special memories. It may be a whole song or just a snippet. For example, I have a vivid childhood memory of running home from school and hearing workmen singing as they renovated a building. I remember the song. It was *Moon River* by Henry Mancini, and the workmen were putting their hearts into it. As I turned the corner, both the moment and the song were gone. They remain in my history, markers on a path that leads in both directions. You, too, will have memories like this. Write down those songs and what they signify for you. When you have more time, choose a triggered memory to explore in more detail.

37

A Bottle on the Beach

*The blue of the bottle was a sudden splinter of colour which
she saw at a distance as she made her way along the beach,
shoulders hunched against the oncoming wind. Its glow
belonged to a different clime, where the sun shone and the sea
was a proper blue. It lay at the tide mark, where the grey mud
met the grey pebbles.*

Karen Liebrich, *The Letter in the Bottle*

Who can resist a bottle on the beach, particularly if it has a
message inside? The one in the above extract contained two locks
of hair and a desperately sad mother's letter, written in French, to
her lost child. Liebrich, a television researcher, was so moved that
she determined to find the mother. Her seven-year quest involved
government departments, the Royal Navy, a private detective, and
even astrologers and tarot readers. Only after the book was
published did Liebrich solve the mystery.

As a motif, messages in bottles have a long and distinguised
history. In 310 BC, the Greek philosopher Theophrastus threw
bottles into the sea to prove that the Mediterranean was formed
by inflow from the Atlantic Ocean. In Elizabethan times, the
English Navy reportedly used bottles to send messages between
ships during the war with Spain. Queen Elizabeth I even
appointed an official 'Uncorker of Ocean Bottles' and made it a
capital offence to open bottles washed ashore. There are sad
stories, too. In 1912, Jeremiah Burke, a passenger on the *Titanic*,

threw a holy water bottle overboard containing a message to his family. It read simply: 'From Titanic, goodbye all, Burke of Glanmire, Cork.' A year later, the bottle washed ashore only a few miles from the young man's home.

Today, if we want to contact someone, all we need do is to pick up our phones. But here's the thing – people still love the idea of putting messages in bottles. You can even buy bottle kits for special occasions and have them sent through the mail instead of throwing them in the ocean. The Valentine's Day kit, for example, comes with a red rose, pink feathers and a scroll printed with your personal message. If you're not bothered about reality, numerous websites offer a virtual bottle-in-the-ocean service. You compose your message, click a button and away it floats into cyberspace, to be picked up by – well, who knows? Not sure what to say? The site has suggestions. Make a wish, send a love letter, get something off your chest, vent your anger, or simply express your feelings. Sounds a bit like therapy but without the hefty bill at the end of the session.

For fiction writers, the message-in-a-bottle theme offers scope for many different kinds of story, both historical and contemporary. The first obvious port of call is love and romance. Nicholas Sparks's *Message in a Bottle* is a classic tear-jerker which begins when a recently divorced woman finds a bottle containing a message of love addressed to *My Dearest Catherine*, and signed *Garrett*. Warner Brothers liked the idea so much they made it into a film, starring Kevin Costner. As with Liebrich's true story, there is mystery involved, but the unfolding narrative is very different. There are plenty of options for you to consider. Suppose the message in the bottle is not romantic? Suppose it's a confession, directions to buried treasure, or the answer to a riddle? What if the bottle doesn't contain a message at all but something else, equally intriguing? Get your creative brain into gear with the following exercise.

THE EXERCISE

Imagine you're walking on the beach one warm sunny morning when you notice something half-buried in the sand. As you get closer, you see it's a bottle with something inside. You open the bottle...

Write for five minutes.

38

Thirteen Ways of Looking at a Blackbird

That's the title of an experimental poem by Wallace Stevens, an American poet who was fascinated by the power of the imagination to transform reality. Reality, he suggests, is a product of our imagination as it shapes the concrete into something that makes sense to us. To demonstrate this idea, he took a concrete image – a blackbird – and wrote a poem containing 13 verses, each one triggered by the quirky ideas and sensations that came to him while thinking about the bird. You can find the whole poem online, but to give you a taste, here's the first verse:

Among twenty snowy mountains,
The only moving thing
Was the eye of the blackbird.

Unlike other poems, which follow a logical progression, the sections of this poem are disconnected. The next verse, for example, compares the human mind to a tree in which three blackbirds sit, leading some to suggest it's a metaphor for Freud's id, ego, and superego. There is, however, no definitive interpretation of any section. Nor does it matter. What's most interesting for us is Stevens' purpose, which is to illustrate that what we 'see' depends on how we look. Perception is a process in which we construct a version of reality rather than being a passive recipient of it. And that construction will be influenced by all sorts of things, including our past experiences, education, cultural values and so on. Stevens' brilliance was in using such a simple image – the blackbird – to highlight the different 'takes'.

The poem continues to intrigue and inspire not just poets and dramatists, but also musicians. The composer David Bruce wrote his piano solo *The Shadow of the Blackbird*, inspired by Stevens' 'shadow' image in the seventh verse: 'If the blackbird in the poem is a mysterious, mystical bird, which is sometimes real, sometimes symbol – it might be god, life or death – then how much more mysterious is its shadow.' In 2011, the piece was performed at Carnegie Hall in New York. Media artist Edward Picot has even produced a Flash animated version of Stevens' poem. The idea came to him one snowy afternoon while gazing through the window at a crab-apple tree, on which perched a blackbird – a startling contrast to the white snow and the red fruit: 'I was immediately reminded of Wallace Stevens' poem, and almost as immediately it occurred to me that the crab-apple tree would make an excellent interface for a new media version, with the bright red apples acting as buttons to call up the different sections.'

Picot's animation is beautiful and fascinating and may give you more insight, both into the poem itself and the power of the imagination. Check it out yourself at edwardpicot.com/thirteenways/

Of course, we don't have to stick with blackbirds. Take anything – a face, a sunset, a painting – and there's a myriad different ways to see it, both literal and metaphorical. As writers, we try to do this as a matter of course. But do we always know how to look? According to art historian James Elkins, whose work focuses on the theory of images in art, science, and nature, we ignore most of what we see because it's just too ordinary. His book, *How to Use Your Eyes*, starts with an admission:

> *It struck me when writing the chapter on grass that if it hadn't been for this book, I might have gone on ignoring grass my whole life. I have sat on grass and mowed it, and have picked it absentmindedly; and I have noticed it in passing when it grows too high on a neighbor's lawn. But before I sat down to write the chapter on grass, I had never really paid attention to it.*

Elkins's book is a wonderful study in how to look at the 'universally unnoticed', including twigs, the markings on a butterfly's wings, stamps, and – my favourite – pavements. We walk on pavements almost every day of our lives but until I read Elkins I had no idea they could crack in so many distinctive ways. While asphalt is prone to *alligator* cracking, cracks on concrete often resemble the craquelure in paintings – which brings a whole new meaning to pavement art. Then we have *thixotropic hardening*, *rutting*, caused by the wheels of cars and trucks, and *shoving*, where the top layer gets pushed. Elkins cites a pavement near Avenue de l'Opéra in Paris which has been pushed *a full five feet down the road, shearing the painted stripes into zigzags.* I've walked past this point in Paris many times and never noticed. Now, thanks to Elkins, I will never forget it. And is that a blackbird I see, on top of the old opera house? Or is it just a trick of the light?

THE EXERCISE

◆ To help you to incorporate the ideas of Stevens, Picot and Elkins into your own work, do a creative search, using 'Looking' as your starting point. If you're artistic, you might even use small pictures instead of words to illustrate your thoughts. Ask yourself silly questions. What does 'looking' look like? How does it feel? Smell? Sound? In one of Stevens' verses, for example, he wonders whether he prefers the sound of the blackbird singing or the moment of silence immediately after. That's the kind of thought that could lead anywhere

◆ Pick an object – natural or man-made – and write your own 13 ways of looking at it. It could be a poem. It could be prose. You choose. Don't feel you have to produce something clever or philosophical. This exercise is about developing mental flexibility and exploring what lies just beyond the obvious. Take a tip from James Elkins who said that when you stop and consider ordinary things, the world 'will gather before your eyes and become thick with meaning'.

39

Watching You Watching Me

When I moved to my present house, I discovered that the previous owners had left a pile of bills unpaid, including ones for a credit card, veterinary services and even a correspondence course. I had no forwarding address and I knew the owners had moved abroad, so I doubt if any of these companies ever received their money.

It started me thinking about honesty and the social codes by which we all live. Research suggests that we alter our behaviour according to cues, such as the risk of being seen – even when that risk is an illusion. A fascinating experiment at Newcastle University found that when a notice with a banner image of eyes was pinned above an honesty box for tea and coffee, the box collected almost three times as much money as it did when the poster featured an image of flowers. According to the researchers, images of eyes induce a perception of being watched and that motivates us to behave less selfishly. Indeed, a later experiment published in *Evolution and Human Behaviour* found that students dropped less litter when they were being 'watched' by a pair of eyes on a poster.

But honesty is not an area where absolutes rule. In one writing class, for example, I was surprised to find that most members saw nothing wrong in being dishonest about their qualifications on a CV. As one student explained: 'Everyone else does it so why should I be at a disadvantage?' It's hard to argue with that kind of reasoning except perhaps on moral grounds. How would we feel, for example, if a surgeon lied about his or her qualifications? Or an airline pilot? Or a childminder?

Such moral questions make honesty and deception perennially popular themes in fiction. In most – but certainly not all – stories, it's part of the unwritten contract between writer and reader that the honest will be rewarded and the dishonest brought to book. However, how we feel about 'dishonest' characters depends in part upon their motivation. In Shakespeare's *Othello,* for example, few would have sympathy with Iago, whose dishonesty is driven by jealousy and paranoia. The tragedy is that Othello chooses to trust the dishonest Iago, rather than Desdemona, his new bride. When Othello realises his mistake – only after he has murdered Desdemona, wrongly believing her to have been unfaithful – he falls on his sword. There are no winners here.

By contrast, in M. C. Beaton's *Agatha Raisin and the Quiche of Death*, Agatha's dishonesty is born of loneliness and a desperate need to make friends in the Cotswold village to which she's just moved. When buying a frozen dinner in the village shop, she sees a poster for a 'Great Quiche Competition':

> *Agatha's mind was racing as she trotted home and shoved the Chicken Korma in the microwave. Wasn't that what mattered in these villages? Being the best at something domestic? Now if she, Agatha Raisin, won that competition, they would sit up and take notice. Maybe ask her to give lectures on her art at the Women's Institute meetings and things like that.*

Agatha can't cook, so she resorts to buying a quiche from a smart deli in London. Unfortunately, the competition judge drops dead after sampling the quiche. Now, not only is she a cheat but – in the eyes of the village – a potential poisoner. There's only one thing to do. At the police interview, she confesses.

We forgive Agatha because we understand that her motives were not malicious or nasty. She has the rest of the book to redeem herself, which she does magnificently by solving the crime. Agatha's weaknesses endear her to her readers, many of whom find the series addictive. Unlike other sleuths, Agatha Raisin is the kind of person we might actually know – flawed and error-prone but immensely likeable.

Now, hands up anyone whose parents told them the ice cream van only plays music when it's run out of ice cream. Ooooh! My father had a different approach. He said that I risked food poisoning owing to the unsanitary conditions on many of the vans. I'm not sure if he really believed this. Parents bend the honesty rules for all sorts of reasons, most of them benign. If they didn't, children would not have the magic of Santa Claus, the tooth fairy, and even Peter Rabbit, who doesn't actually wear a blue coat or drink camomile tea. Such small deceptions are part of the landscape of childhood. Arguably, so, too, are those designed to protect children from knowledge that might be too shocking or stressful for immature minds.

When we grow up, it's a different matter. When those close to us hide the truth or distort it in the name of protection, they often set in motion a tidal wave of unpredictable consequences. This is rich hunting ground for fiction writers. *The Memory Keeper's Daughter* by Kim Edwards is a good example. Set in Kentucky in 1964, the book opens in a snowstorm, during which Dr David Henry's wife, Norah, gives birth to twins, aided only by her husband and a nurse. One of the babies has Down's syndrome.

Haunted by memories of his own sister's early death from a heart defect, David decides to spare Norah the anguish of raising a child with a short life expectancy. Instead, he asks the nurse to take the baby to a mental institution. In the less enlightened 1960s, that was the fate of many such children. He tells Norah that the baby is dead.

Needless to say, things go awry from that moment on, and David's dishonesty can never be undone. Was his decision a 'shocking act of betrayal' as some have suggested? Or was it an example of what can happen when someone under stress makes a snap decision? Dishonesty comes in many flavours, some of them sweet, some of them sour, some wrapped up in a whole raft of baggage. The wonderful thing about writing is that we can explore as many flavours as we like. One thing's for sure. Absolute honesty is rarely possible, nor even desirable. We don't really want to know that someone hated a present we gave them or that someone else thinks we're a bore or that our laugh sounds like a train going into a tunnel. As Jane Austen remarks in Emma: *Seldom, very seldom, does complete truth belong to any human disclosure; seldom can it happen that something is not a little disguised or a little mistaken.*

THE EXERCISE

◆ What does honesty mean to you? Is honesty always the best policy or are there occasions when it's OK to lie? Have you ever discovered that someone you trusted has lied to you? Have you ever lied to protect someone else? Explore your thoughts in a creative search.

◆ Choose one of the following characters to inspire the beginning of a story.
  – A character who is a compulsive liar;
  – A character who is dishonest with money;

- A character who does something dishonest on impulse;
- A character who is dishonest about their past;
- A character who tells a lie to protect someone else;
- A character who believes that being honest is more important than being kind;
- A character who lies because they are afraid.

◆ Write for five minutes, using the following sentence as a trigger: *It all started with the smallest of white lies.*

40

Exits and Entrances

Exit, pursued by a bear.

William Shakespeare, *The Winter's Tale*

Years ago, when I was doing A Level English, we all chortled when we came to the above stage direction in *The Winter's Tale*. Did Shakespeare intend it to be funny? No one knows for sure. Perhaps, as some critics have suggested, the bard was simply trying to give the audience a taste of the sensational. It certainly adds drama to what might otherwise have been a piece of dull reportage: 'Oh, have you heard? Antigonus is dead. Yes, savaged by a bear. Methinks his legs were not in good repair.'

In novels and short stories, we don't have to grapple with stage directions but exits and entrances are still psychological hot spots, ideal points at which to introduce dramatic tension. Think of airports. Whether you're in London, Heathrow or Brisbane, Australia, you find the same sea of expectant faces outside the arrivals hall, waiting for passengers to exit the no-man's-land of baggage collection and passport control. And when the right face or faces appear, there's that flash of recognition and hugs all round. The exit has become an entrance to the landside world.

Exits and entrances are moments in space and time at which our past intersects with our future, both literally and psychologically. It's perhaps hardly surprising that the most memorable moments in fiction are often scenes in which characters meet, are reunited or are thrust apart by circumstance and must say goodbye. We all have our favourites. It might be the heartbreaking sequence in *Titanic* when Jack makes Rose promise never to let go, before he dies in the icy sea. Jack's final words give strength to Rose and she fulfils her promise by living life to the full, before the two are finally reunited. It might be the *Doctor Who* episode in which another Rose – Rose Tyler – says goodbye to the Doctor on the sand at Bad Wolf Bay. She reappears in later episodes, having found a way to move between worlds. It might even be Scarlett O'Hara's last scene with Rhett when he finally decides that he's had enough:

> *'Scarlett, when you are forty-five, perhaps you will know what I'm talking about and then perhaps you, too, will be tired of imitation gentry and shoddy manners and cheap emotions. But I doubt it. I think you'll always be more attracted by glister than by gold. Anyway, I can't wait that long to see.'*

On the next page he tells her he doesn't give a damn. And the entrance? Well, for Scarlett, it's Tara, the antebellum mansion to which she turns for comfort:

> *She had gone back to Tara once in fear and defeat and she had emerged from its sheltering walls, strong and armed for victory. What she had done once, somehow – please God, she could again!*

The final words point to the future: *Tomorrow is another day.*

You might also want to check out the goodbye scene between Ashley Wilkes and Scarlett, in which she gives him a fringed sash, tied with a love knot to bring him luck as he goes off to fight in the Civil War. Novelist Cathy Elliott has drawn attention to similarities between that scene and one in the second series of *Downton Abbey* in which Lady Mary meets Matthew at the railway station and offers him her good luck charm, a stuffed toy, as he leaves to go to war.

Which brings us to *Casablanca*. Not only does *Casablanca* have a great 'entrance' scene in which Ilsa, Rick's lost love, asks the cafe's pianist to play *As Time Goes By* to alert Rick to her presence, but it also has one of the best farewell scenes in the history of cinema. The setting is a foggy night in that classic entry and exit zone, an airport in Morocco during World War II. Ilsa's war hero husband Laszlo must board a plane to escape from the Nazis. Will Ilsa go with him? Or will she stay with Rick? The power of the scene is that we just can't decide what the best resolution is. In the end, Rick makes the sacrifice. Laszlo needs her, he tells Ilsa. If the plane leaves without her, she'll regret it for the rest of her life. 'But what about us?' Ilsa asks. Rick replies, 'We'll always have Paris. We didn't have, we lost it, but we got it back when you came to Casablanca.'

Through the airport fog, the plane's engine propellers begin to spin. Ilsa's eyes brim with tears as she looks at Rick for the last time. 'Goodbye, Rick,' she says. 'God bless you.' And we know then that Rick has done the right thing. Not only has he 'got back' Paris but also the Self that was damaged by the earlier separation. Now he can move forward.

It's a fine exit scene, but *Casablanca* is more than fine. It's a great film. In the final shot, we get a glimpse – just a flicker – of the future, which turns the exit into an entrance. Captain Louis Renault, Vichy France's prefect of police, renounces his allegiance to the Third Reich. Instead of arresting Rick for holding him at gunpoint, he and Rick forge a new alliance, for the Allied Cause. 'Louis,' Rick says, as they leave the airport together, 'I think this is the beginning of a beautiful friendship.'

THE EXERCISE

◆ Think of the exits and entrances in your own life, the meetings, the partings, the greetings and the farewells. Which ones stick in your mind? In what way — or ways — were any of them entrances as well as exits? Choose one to explore in a five-minute freewrite.

◆ Write a scene in which two characters say goodbye to each other. It could be a temporary parting or it could be permanent. Who are these characters? What are the circumstances? Are they sad or happy? Is one sad and the other happy? Will either learn anything from the parting? What happens at the parting that points to the future?

41

Make a Wish

At Yoko Ono's 2012 exhibition 'To the Light', which showed at London's Serpentine Gallery, visitors were invited to write down their wishes and pin them to a tree outside. Growing up in Japan, Ono remembers tying her own wishes to a tree in the temple courtyard where the branches were so full of wishes they looked like white flower blossom. Now, it's something she incorporates into all her exhibitions, encouraging people to write their messages for peace and tie them to a tree branch.

Wishing trees have grown in popularity over recent years. However, trees have always been associated with magical powers. The Druids created sacred oak-tree groves and from earliest times people believed that you could make a wish come true by touching a sacred tree, or – in some cases – by making a votive offering to the spirit who lived in it. On the Portmeirion Estate in Wales, seven felled trees were found to have large numbers of coins pushed into their trunks. According to estate manager Meurig Jones, the practice dates back to the 1700s when a sick person might stick a coin in the tree to cure their illness.

But our love of making wishes is not limited to trees. Who has not made a wish after tossing a coin into a fountain, blowing out candles on a birthday cake or breaking a chicken wishbone? This fascination is reflected in fiction, where wishes – making them, granting them, misusing them – are classic motifs. Think of Aladdin from *The Tales of the Arabian Nights,* Enid Blyton's

Adventures of the Wishing Chair, or the many versions of Grimm's *Three Wishes* in which a woodcutter finds that sticking sausages on noses is not a good idea. Although we think of such stories as just good fun, most do carry the underlying message that wishing can be risky. In Edith Nesbit's *Five Children and It*, for example, a sand fairy can grant one wish a day but most of the wishes turn into disasters because the children simply haven't thought things through. When a man is blamed for stealing jewels that the children 'wished' belonged to their mother, the children realise that it's time to call it a day.

In Alexandra Potter's romantic comedy *Be Careful What You Wish For*, Heather Hamilton is careful to stress that her wishes are for ordinary, everyday things, *not great big life-changing wishes – like discovering Brad Pitt's shooting his latest blockbuster in my neighbourhood.* She starts to make a 'wish' list, including ice cream with no calories, anti-wrinkle creams that work, and meeting *a man whose hobbies include washing-up, monogamy and foreplay.* It's predictable 30-something's angst but it's fun and, as a character-revealing device, it works a treat. Things move up a gear after Heather buys a bunch of heather from a gypsy and finds that all her little wishes start coming true. However, like the children in *Five Children and It,* she soon realises that getting what you want doesn't always make you happy.

For something altogether more sinister, *The Monkey's Paw* by W. W. Benson is a short story which gave me nightmares when I first read it. It's a horror classic which has been adapted numerous times for radio, stage, and screen. The monkey's paw of the title is a mummified object brought back from India. Its owner, a soldier, shows it to a friend and his family one stormy night:

'It had a spell put on it by an old Fakir,' said the Sergeant-Major, 'a very holy man. He wanted to show that fate ruled people's lives, and that those who interfered with it did so to their sorrow. He put a spell on it so that three separate men could each have three wishes from it.'

Ah, those three wishes again. Will they never die? Probably not – they make such good copy. Needless to say, the soldier's friend can't resist. The story is out of copyright and available online, so check it out. Unlike some of the screen adaptations, the final chill in the original takes place mainly in the reader's own imagination – something that's amazingly effective and worth remembering if you decide to head down the horror route in your own writing.

As with all popular themes, it's a good idea to find an unusual angle if you want to sell your story. Most 'wish' narratives focus on the person making the wish. Few consider the entity – the tree spirit, the fairy, the genie – who grants the wishes. *Je Souhaite* from Season 7 of the *X Files* series is a brilliant exception. The genie – Jenn – gained her powers after wishing for great power and long life from another genie. Jenn's attitude to granting wishes reflects her annoyance at having to spend the rest of her life doing other people's bidding. When Agent Mulder asks for world peace, for example, she responds by wiping out the entire population. Mulder has to use the second of his three wishes to restore it. Instead of wasting his final wish, he asks Jenn what she would wish for in his place. Jenn replies that she'd like to live her life moment by moment – enjoying it for what it is instead of worrying about what isn't: 'I'd sit down somewhere with a great cup of coffee and I'd watch the world go by.'

The story ends with Jenn sitting in a coffee shop on a street in Washington DC. As she watches people walking past the window, the waitress brings her a cup of coffee. Jenn looks happy and we realise that Mulder has used his last wish to set her free.

THE EXERCISE

◆ You find a rather unusual object in a charity shop. You buy it, take it home, but when you try to clean it, there's a puff of smoke and a genie appears. The genie says you have three wishes. What happens next?

◆ Write your own everyday 'wish' list. When you've finished, look at your list and see what it reveals about you as a person. Next time you're struggling with a character who refuses to come alive, try creating a wish list for them.

◆ Begin a story using the following first-line trigger: *I used to like trees but that was before I found the Wishing Tree.*

$$\text{(42)}$$

Cellar Door Beauty

In *The Bridges of Madison County* by Robert James Waller, photographer Robert Kincaid has come to Madison Country to shoot the famous covered bridges. He loves his work and he also loves language. He does not just hear words; he experiences them:

> *'Blue' was one of his favourite words. He liked the feeling it made on his lips and tongue as he said it. Words have physical feeling, not just meaning, he remembered thinking when he was young. He liked other words, such as 'distant', 'woodsmoke', 'highway', 'ancient', 'passage', 'voyageur' and 'India' for how they sounded, how they tasted and what they conjured up in his mind.*

Kincaid keeps lists of words he likes and posts them up in his room. Sometimes, he joins the words into phrases and pins them up too, like miniature poems. In the context of the book, Kincaid's response to language helps to characterise him as a man who is intellectually and emotionally sensitive. When Francesca Johnson, an Iowan farmer's wife who was born in Italy, falls in love with Kincaid, we understand why. She, whose everyday life revolves around the farm, thirsts for conversation about art and dreams. Kincaid quenches that thirst. He tells her about his work, explaining that while amateur photographers 'take' pictures, he 'makes' them. When he's finished with a bridge, he says, he will have made it into something that expresses the poetry in the image.

As a photographer and musician himself, Waller's own sensory sensitivity is reflected in the character of Robert Kincaid. Indeed, the whole novel has the sensuous quality of a piece of art or a haunting orchestral melody. Waller prepares us for this in the very first line: *There are songs that come free from the blue-eyed grass, from the dust of a thousand country roads. This is one of them.*

This appreciation of words for their sensory qualities is not peculiar to Waller. J. R. R. Tolkien once talked about the 'simpler, deeper-rooted' and 'more immediate' phonetic pleasure of words, citing 'cellar door' as having a beauty quite separate from its meaning. The linguist J. R. Firth even coined the term 'phonoaesthetics' to refer to the aesthetic properties of language and its sound sequences. For example, *sl-* is associated with slipperiness and smoothness, as in slip, slide, slime, slither, and slick. However, its sensory qualities transfer to other words whose literal meaning is neither slippery nor smooth, such as slim, sloe, sleigh, sleep and sly, which has a metaphorical 'slipperiness'.

Of course, the words we like will always have a personal element as well as a linguistic one. I'm not sure about Tolkien's 'cellar door', but some of his place names – Lothlorien, Rivendell, Bucklebury – have a euphonic, almost magical appeal for me, and probably for anyone who has read the books or seen the *Lord of the Rings* films. My own list, however, might include other words, such as driftwood, spearmint, Arapahoe and indigo. Language is full of words that appeal to us because of their sound, their taste and the images they evoke in our imaginations. Explore your own associations in the following exercise.

THE EXERCISE

Create your own collection of 'cellar door' words. When you've finished, you might like to follow Robert Kincaid's example of joining some of your words into phrases, incorporating them in a poem, or using them in a short prose piece. In *The Bridges of Madison County,* Waller combines almost Kincaid's entire list of words in a paragraph that sparkles with sensory detail. For copyright reasons, I cannot quote it, but if you'd like to read it yourself, it's on page 107 of the Arrow Books imprint by Random House.

$$\left(43\right)$$

Motive for Murder

In Agatha Christie's *Hallowe'en Party*, Poirot asks one of the suspects to tell him what the murder victim was like. When the suspect replies, *'She was – how can I put it? – not important. She had rather an ugly voice. Shrill. Really that's about all I remember about her,'* Poirot pounces. Do you mean, he says, that she was not interesting? The suspect agrees and Poirot retorts: *'It is my view that people devoid of interest are unlikely to be murdered. People are murdered for gain, for fear or for love. One takes one's choice but one has to have a starting point –'*

Indeed one does. The motive in *Hallowe'en Party* is fear: fear of what the victim might be able to reveal. I won't say more in case it spoils the story for you. This is one of Christie's last novels and while it may not be in the same league as some of her earlier successes, such as *The Murder of Roger Ackroyd*, it's still a good read. And what better starting point for a writer than the motive for murder? Try the exercise.

THE EXERCISE

Pick whichever motive appeals to you the most – gain, fear or love – and write as many examples as you can in five minutes. For instance, if you've chosen love, ask yourself, 'Who loves whom? Why might love of that person – or indeed thing – drive someone to murder? It might be revenge for a past hurt to the loved one. It might be something else. Let your imagination run wild.

44

Travelling in Time

Sometimes it feels as though your attention has wandered for just an instant. Then, with a start, you realize that the book you were holding, the red plaid cotton shirt with white buttons, the favorite black jeans and the maroon socks with an almost-hole in one heel, the living room, the about-to-whistle tea kettle in the kitchen: all of these have vanished.

Audrey Niffenegger, *The Time Traveler's Wife*

This is Henry DeTamble explaining how it feels to travel in time. Henry is not a willing traveller. He's a librarian who suffers from what the author calls 'chrono-impairment', a rare condition in which his genetic clock resets itself and, without any warning, periodically catapults him into the future or back into his past. The author's medicalisation of time travel is an imaginative touch. This is not a sci-fi adventure. It's a love story about ordinary people, trying to have a normal relationship. The time travel is the obstacle, the problem, the source of the conflict. That's a neat twist.

When did we humans become fascinated by time travel? According to one bright spark, it probably happened at a party when someone drank too much, insulted their boss and told him precisely what was wrong with the company. Certainly that may help to explain its appeal in fiction where the idea of going back in time to avert disaster in the future is irresistible, particularly at the box office. Think of the *Terminator* films or *Back to the Future,* in which Marty McFly, having accidentally prevented his own parents from meeting, must travel back in time – or cease to exist. I've seen this film so many times but when the lightning strikes the clock tower and that fabulous DeLorean starts to burn rubber, my knuckles go white.

But back to reality. *The Clock That Went Backward* by Edward Page Mitchell is usually regarded as the first story to involve a machine in time travel – in this case an eight-foot-high 16th-century Dutch clock. However, H. G. Wells's *The Time Machine,* published in 1895, is the one that captured the public imagination. Today, the iconic machine is of course Doctor Who's TARDIS. It may not be as cool as Marty McFly's DeLorean, but it saw most of us through our childhoods, albeit from behind the sofa. One day, a brave soul will invent a brilliant new time machine – it might even be you – but most writers simply look for other ways to send their characters whizzing through time.

Fortunately, time travel themes were present in fiction long before the invention of machines and these early stories make good source material. The characters in these stories are mostly accidental travellers, whose transportation starts after falling asleep, taking a narcotic, or receiving an injury that knocks them out. One well-known example is Washington Irving's *Rip Van Winkle,* published in 1819, but stories in which characters lose consciousness and wake up years into the future or the past exist in many cultural myths. In 1843, Charles Dickens adapted the 'falling asleep' theme for Scrooge's trips to Christmas past and Christmas 'yet to come'. And let's not forget Mark Twain's *A Connecticut Yankee in King Arthur's Court,* in which an engineer is hit on the head with a crowbar and wakes up under an oak tree in sixth-century Camelot where his knowledge of technology astonishes the locals.

These methods of time travel are still hot, constantly revived, reworked and reinterpreted by contemporary authors who adapt them to suit the current zeitgeist. At the height of the 1960s drug culture, for example, Daphne du Maurier wrote *The House on the Strand,* in which the main character takes an experimental substance that whisks him back to the 14th century. Similarly, you may recognise the Connecticut Yankee's bang on the head in the television series *Life on Mars* in which policeman Sam Tyler is hit by a car and transported back to the 1970s. In the sequel, *Ashes to Ashes,* a policewoman, Alex Drake, is shot and goes back to the 1980s. It may not be Camelot but it was an excuse for some large helpings of nostalgia, including the famous orange car, which gave rise to the catchphrase 'Fire up the Quattro'.

For those of you who want to give your characters more control over their time travel, portals are popular. Characters usually stumble upon these by accident, but then nip back and forth, which gives their creators lots of opportunities for intriguing plot development. For example, in the 1990s sitcom *Goodnight Sweetheart*, Gary Sparrow, a television repairman, walks down an alley called Duckett's Passage and finds himself in wartime London where he establishes a second life, pretending to be a secret agent. Like Twain's Connecticut Yankee, Gary uses his knowledge of the future to impress the locals. As the two lives interact, his status and confidence in his first life start to improve. It's a brilliant blend of nostalgia, fantasy and gritty reality, all wrapped up in a comedy cloak.

Portals are useful for children's fiction, too, where it could be scary for young readers to find themselves stranded. In Philippa Pearce's Carnegie Medal winner *Tom's Midnight Garden,* the portal is a real door in an old house since converted into flats.

During the day, the door opens onto a dull backyard but at midnight Tom finds an enchanted garden which belonged to the house before its conversion. It's a magical story about friendship, memories and growing up. Portals can be anything from a circle of light behind a character's chair, as in Robert Heinlein's short story *By his Bootstraps*, to an antique taxi that arrives at midnight and transports the character from 21st-century Paris to the Left Bank in the 1920s. That's from Woody Allen's *Midnight in Paris*, starring Owen Wilson as a Hollywood writer travelling back in time to meet Ernest Hemingway, Cole Porter and Gertrude Stein, who kindly gives him some help with his new screenplay. It's a light and frothy film but it's also funny and romantic and it does have a serious point to make about looking at the past through rose-tinted glasses.

Of course, nostalgia is part of the human condition and one reason perhaps why we enjoy stories with a time travel flavour, even if we're not sci-fi fans. As scientist Richard Lenski points out, we time travel in our memories every moment of our lives, mentally recalling people, places and events, and that is often pleasurable. Paul J. Nahin argues that time travel stories fascinate us because they make us think. Certainly, time travel stories offer us the opportunity to think outside the box, even if we don't always manage to solve the problem. For writers, Nahin's book *Time Machines: Time Travel in Physics, Metaphysics, and Science Fiction*, is an excellent source of inspiration – if not always an easy read. The first chapters offer a comprehensive review of existing time travel literature and film, while the section on time travel paradoxes will give you lots of ideas that you can develop.

In the meantime, try the exercise.

In 1921 Lord Dunsany wrote a play called *If*, in which a businessman receives a magic crystal that allows him to go back in time and change just one event. He's happy with his current life, but ten years ago, he missed a train under annoying circumstances. He decides to go back and catch it...

◆ If you could go back in time and change just one event in your own life, what would it be? How might your life have been different as a result of this change?

◆ Suppose the crystal will allow you to visit any time in history or the future. What time would you choose? Where would you go?

◆ Create a character (any age, any historical period) who finds a time travel portal in an unexpected place. Where is the portal, where does it lead and what happens to the character? Freewrite for five minutes.

45

Snippet Trigger – Guilt

This is the first snippet trigger I gave to my writing class students. The story appeared in my local free newspaper under the caption: *'I swiped your sweets, Father' culprit owns up after 68 years*. The 'culprit' was a 78-year-old man who took two pieces of Toblerone chocolate from his scoutmaster – an Anglican priest – during a camping trip. In a letter to the scoutmaster, enclosing a cheque for £50, he wrote that he had carried the guilt with him for nearly 70 years and could no longer live with the shame. Poor man. I hope he felt better afterwards.

In terms of emotion, guilt is one of the biggies. 'Nothing is more wretched than the mind of a man conscious of guilt,' wrote the Roman playwright Plautus. He is right. We talk of guilt 'gnawing' at our conscience, 'eating' at our soul. The dramatist Nicholas Rowe called it a fiend, the avenging fiend 'that follows us behind, with whips and stings'. Shakespeare uses it to bring down Macbeth; John Steinbeck uses it in East of Eden to whip – and later redeem – Cal after he reveals to his younger brother, Aron, that their mother was a prostitute. More recently Ian McEwan uses it to torment Bryony in *Atonement*.

Why does guilt work so well in fiction? According to Anaïs Nin, guilt is a burden we can't bear alone. In her erotic novel *A Spy in the House of Love*, Sabina phones a stranger – the lie detector – in the middle of the night. The lie detector correctly divines the reason for the call. There is, he tells her, *only one relief: to confess, to be caught, tried, punished*:

> *'That's the ideal of every criminal. But it's not quite so simple. Only half of the self wants to atone, to be freed of the torments of guilt. The other half of man wants to continue to be free. So only half of the self surrenders, calling out "catch me" while the other half creates obstacles, difficulties, seeks to escape. It's a flirtation with justice. If justice is nimble it will follow the clue with the criminal's help. If not, the criminal will take care of his own atonement.'*

In Shakespeare's *Macbeth,* this psychological conflict is symbolised by blood, the 'stain' of which neither Macbeth nor his wife can wipe from their hands. Although Macbeth does the killing, and is tormented by Banquo's ghost, Lady Macbeth is complicit in the crimes. At first, she seems icily calm, telling Macbeth that a *little water clears us of this deed.* Later, in a classic example of Anaïs Nin's 'catch me' behaviour, she begins to sleepwalk, rubbing her hands and crying *Out, damn'd spot! out, I say!* But it will not go away: *Here's the smell of the blood still: all the perfumes of Arabia will not sweeten this little hand.* Eventually, the guilt is too much for her and she commits suicide – thereby taking care of her own atonement.

Of course, we don't have to write tragedies to make use of guilt. According to psychologists, guilt can be a positive force for change. In *Personal Narratives about Guilt,* Roy F. Baumeister *et al.,* found that 'Guilt makes people learn lessons and alter their subsequent behaviour so as to avoid repetition of harmful acts.' Furthermore, if guilt motivates a person to confess and apologise, the way is open for forgiveness and redemption. That might not

SNIPPET TRIGGER — GUILT / 165

have worked for Lord and Lady Macbeth but it does for Cal in *East of Eden.*

As a theme, guilt – and its companion, shame – make excellent story triggers. Both are emotions. Consequently, everyone can relate to them. Who has not felt guilt at some time in their lives? Try the exercise.

- Use guilt as the focus of a creative search. Remember that guilt comes in many different flavours: guilt about things we've done, guilt about things we haven't done, guilt about thoughts we feel we 'ought' not to have, and guilt imposed on us by others. In *Scripts People Live,* for example, Claude Steiner points to parents as a major source of guilt: 'Guilt,' he says, 'prevents children from striving for the things that they want but which their parents do not want them to have.' I imagine that many parents would like to put forward a different point of view. If that's you, go ahead. It's your call.

- Write about a character whose past contains a guilty secret. What is the secret, what is its context and how does it affect the character's life?

46

Crunch Points

In his book *Decisions, Decisions: the Art of Effective Decision Making*, David A. Welch points out that all decisions have three parts. First, you identify your goal. Second, you identify your options. And third, you choose from among your options. Even the most trivial decision – such as buying a bottle of orange juice in a convenience store – fits this pattern.

As writers, we have to help our characters make their choices, and if we're cautious ourselves in real life, we might find that tricky. Decisions can have far-reaching consequences and none of us wants to wreck our future. But fiction beats to a different drum. When characters choose the 'wrong' path, it only adds to the conflict and heightens tension. What matters in fiction is keeping the action alive.

Keep in mind, too, that sometimes tiny, almost insignificant choices can have big consequences. 'You leave a cinema, but forget your raincoat. You go back and find in the next seat your future wife.' The playwright Alan Ayckbourn once gave that example of how a single moment can change our lives. Similarly, in retrospect, poor choices can turn into good ones. For example, if you have dinner in a dodgy restaurant and choose a dish containing poultry, you might get salmonella poisoning. Big mistake? Perhaps not. If you have to stay away from work next day, you won't be driving your car along a stretch of road where someone happens to be using their mobile phone while trying to

CRUNCH POINTS / 167

overtake. You avoid the pile-up in which you would have been involved. It's a funny old world.

So, don't be afraid of decisions in stories. They keep the plot moving.

THE EXERCISE

Choose one of the following options and write for five minutes:

◆ Thinking about your own life, what have been your most difficult decisions?

◆ If you could go back in time and change just one decision, what might it be?

◆ To explore the idea that tiny, almost insignificant choices can change the direction of our lives, write about a character who hears their landline telephone ringing as they leave the house for work. Do they answer the phone? Or do they ignore it, on the assumption that the caller will call their mobile if it's important? Explore both paths.

47

First Line Magic

Have you ever chosen to read a novel because the first line appealed to you? Years ago, when I had a toddler to look after, I'd go to the library, pull books off the shelves, and choose three based almost solely on whether the opening line grabbed me. If I was lucky I could be out of the building before my daughter demolished a craft display. It might not have been the best way to pick a book, but it introduced me to authors I might never have tried if I'd had more time. It also taught me the power of an opening to reel in the reader. That came in handy when I began to write my own fiction. I knew that a busy editor with a slush pile would be more likely to read my work if the first line caught her attention. Later, I went to a conference at which two editors talked of 'holding their breath' if the first line intrigued them. I knew I was on to something.

But what makes an intriguing opening line? Authors use a variety of techniques. We're all familiar with the fast-action *he-opened-the-door-and-the-bomb-went-off* type of opener. It's reliable, but there are other options. Here are some for you to try.

THE VISCERAL
Visceral first lines appeal to the senses more than the intellect. They encourage the reader to feel, as in this one from Audrey Schulman's *The Cage*:

Beryl holds an ice cube in her hand as she sits in her closet.

Here Schulman raises a question: why would anyone want to sit in a closet holding an ice cube? We have to read on to discover that Beryl is a wildlife photographer, preparing for an expedition to the Arctic to photograph polar bears. However, the ice is key to the line's success. I'm writing this on one of the hottest days of the year but I can *feel* that melting cube in my palm. You can use other senses to achieve a similar effect. Here are three to whet your appetite:

We came in on the wind of the carnival. A warm wind for February, laden with the hot greasy scents of frying pancakes and sausages and powdery-sweet waffles...
Joanne Harris, *Chocolat*

The scent and smoke and sweat of a casino are nauseating at three in the morning.
Ian Fleming, *Casino Royale*

The snow started to fall several hours before her labor began.
Kim Edwards, *The Memory Keeper's Daughter*

THE STARTLE STATEMENT

Every newspaper and magazine editor knows the importance of a striking lead to attract the wandering reader's eye. In a piece of fiction, the startle statement achieves the same purpose. It's a popular choice with many best-selling authors:

The strangest thing about my wife's return from the dead was how other people reacted.
Anne Tyler, *The Beginner's Goodbye*

Jail is not as bad as you imagine.

Anna Quindlen, *One True Thing*

*Someone once told me that, in France alone, a quarter of a
million letters are delivered every year to the dead.*

Joanne Harris, *Peaches for Monsieur le Curé*

These sentences are designed to pique the reader's curiosity.
People have busy lives, which they don't want to waste. A quirky
opener won't hold a reader's interest indefinitely, but it will buy
you time; time to persuade the reader that your story is worth
reading.

THE TIME ANCHOR

*At one o'clock in the morning, Carl, the night porter, turned
down the last of three table lamps in the main lobby of the
Windermere Hotel.*

Raymond Chandler, *I'll be Waiting*

At first glance, starting with time might seem a bit dull. However,
our lives are structured according to time, both in small chunks –
the time of day – and larger slices like the time of year and the
changing seasons. When we use time – and time-associated words
like 'autumn', 'Tuesday' and 'sunset' – we ground the story in
something that has immediate meaning for the reader. Thriller
writers often open with time to give a sense of tension:

*Five minutes to three in the afternoon. Exactly sixty-one hours
before it happened.*

Lee Child, *61 Hours*

Time-anchored openings are versatile. Use them straight, as in Lee Child's example or mix and match with other types. In *The Prisoner of Heaven,* Carlos Ruiz Zaphon adds sensory detail to create the feel of Christmas:

> *That year at Christmas time, every morning dawned laced with frost under leaden skies.*

In the short story *Murder of a Gypsy King,* Edward D. Hoch uses time – and place – to enhance a moment of psychological transition:

> *On the long, lonely highway into Bucharest that sunny August afternoon, Jennifer Beatty suddenly changed her mind.*

Still looking for inspiration? How about the philosophical opener:

> *Everything comes to an end. A good bottle of wine, a summer's day, a long-running sitcom, one's life and eventually our species.*
>
> Jasper Fforde, *The Woman who Died a Lot*

Or the question:

> *Why was it, Tiffany Aching wondered, that people liked noise so much?*
>
> Terry Pratchett, *I Shall Wear Midnight*

THE EXERCISE

Make a list of the different types of first line and write examples of each, as many as you can in the time you have available. You will probably find that certain openings appeal to you, while others leave you cold. Choose the ones that you enjoy writing and practise those. When you need inspiration for a new story, use one of your openers as a trigger.

Coming Home

'Home to stay, Glory! Yes!' her father said, and her heart sank. He attempted a twinkle of joy at this thought, but his eyes were damp with commiseration. 'To stay for a while this time!' he amended, and took her bag from her, shifting his cane to his weaker hand. Dear God, she thought, dear God in heaven. So began and ended all her prayers these days, which were really cries of amazement. How could her father be so frail?

Marilynne Robinson, *Home*

In the above extract, 38-year-old Glory Boughton returns to Gilead in Iowa to look after her dying father. The youngest of eight children, Glory grew up in a house bursting with life. Now, with her mother dead and her siblings absent, she is dismayed to find her childhood home has lost its heart. The oak tree in the garden, which once had four swings hanging from its branches, still flourishes, but the front porch is overrun with trumpet vines, and the coppice, once alive with games of hide-and-seek, is desolate. Soon, Glory is joined by her brother Jack, the family's black sheep, hoping to make peace with the father who loves him. For both Glory and Jack, the old home becomes a place of refuge, where the pains of the past can rise to the surface like thorns to be extracted.

Winner of the 2009 Orange Prize for fiction, *Home* is a novel about families, relationships and healing, as well as pain. It follows a tradition of powerful stories, whose theme is 'Returning Home'. Such stories strike a universal chord. In the Indian epic *Ramayana*, Prince Rama is banished to the forest for 14 years before being allowed to return home and claim his rightful place on the throne. In Homer's *Odyssey*, the warrior Odysseus returns from Troy to reclaim his wife and his threatened home on Ithaca. In children's fiction, Edith Nesbit's *The Railway Children* tells the story of children whose father is bundled off to prison, after being wrongly convicted of selling state secrets. His return at the end, both in the book and on film, where smoke from the train slowly clears to reveal him, is a classic tear-jerker. Choked with happiness, the children rush him back to 'Three Chimneys', where he stands in the garden, marvelling at the flowers, each one a miracle after the flagstones and gravel of the prison yard:

> *Now the house door opens. Bobbie's voice calls: 'Come in, Daddy; come in!' He goes in and the door is shut. I think we will not open the door or follow him. I think that just now we are not wanted there. I think it will be best for us to go quickly and quietly away. At the end of the field, among the thin gold spikes of grass and the harebells and Gipsy roses and St. John's Wort, we may just take one last look, over our shoulders, at the white house where neither we nor anyone else is wanted now.*

Sometimes, as in *The Railway Children,* the return is a joyful occasion, sometimes it's forced upon the characters by circumstances beyond their control, as in *Home,* but whatever the context, homecoming always has consequences. Caryl Phillips's post-colonial novel *State of Independence* highlights the difficulty of returning to your homeland after a long absence. The main character, Bertram Francis, left his home on St Kitts 20 years ago

to study in England. When he returns, slightly anxious but
expecting a warm welcome, he's dismayed to find that he no
longer belongs. His beloved younger brother is dead. His friends
don't want to know him. Even the weather makes him sweat, itch
and smell in his British clothes.

Bertram's experience mirrors that of many returning after a long
absence only to find that they have become outsiders in the place
they call home. The old reality is gone, replaced by something that
doesn't match the mental image. In *Imaginary Homelands*, Salman
Rushdie talks about the sense of loss felt by those disconnected
from their roots and his own urge, as a writer, to reclaim the
India of his past *not in the faded greys of old family-album
snapshots but whole, in CinemaScope and glorious Technicolor*. But
at the same time, Rushdie acknowledges that physical absence
from a homeland means that when we do try to recall it, we can
never do it precisely. Instead, what we create is *fictions, not actual
cities or villages but invisible ones, imaginary homelands*.

Of course, it could be argued that with the world now a global
village and many families fragmented across different continents
'home' is no longer the place where we were born. Nevertheless,
for many – perhaps most – people, there's a desire to recreate the
'home' culture in an alien environment. Chinatown in San
Francisco, for example, began in 1848 with just two men and one
woman. Now, it's home to the largest Chinese community outside
Asia. Similarly, there are Jewish quarters, little Italys, even – in
Spain – little Britains, where communities of retirees drink gin
and tonic by the pool. Why do we do this? Maya Angelou, the
celebrated African American writer and civil rights activist, thinks
she has the answer. In *Letter To My Daughter,* she writes: *I
believe that one can never leave home. I believe that one carries the*

shadows, the dreams, the fears and the dragons of home under one's skin, at the extreme corners of one's eyes and possibly in the gristle of the earlobe.

What do you think? What does home mean to you? Is it, as Angelou suggests, already in you, or is it something that you create; a place of inner peace, a state of mind? Explore your ideas in the following exercise.

THE EXERCISE

Choose one of the following options:

◆ Do a five-minute freewrite, using 'home' as your trigger.

◆ In your mind, create your perfect 'home'. Where will it be? Remember, this is fantasy so there are no rules. It could be a cabin on the beach, with bleached wooden floors and white shutters on the windows, a tree-house set high among the branches of a giant redwood, or perhaps a barge, moving slowly up the longest (fantasy) river in the world. Fill your perfect home with sounds, scents and textures to bring it alive. If you want another person or people there, feel free. It's your place. When everything is perfect, write it down before you lose it.

◆ Here are some novels with 'home' in the title. Titles are designed to be evocative for readers and they often make interesting triggers for a freewrite. Take one of these titles and see where it leads you – maybe the start of a story? (I've deliberately omitted the authors so as not to influence you. If you want more, enter 'Home' into Amazon.co.uk)

The Road Home	*Far From Home*	*Broken Home*
Home Before Dark	*Come Home*	*Never Coming Home*
The Girl Who Came Home	*Too Close to Home*	*Home for the Summer*
On the Way Home	*Home for Christmas*	*Writing Home*
Home is a long time ago	*Music from Home*	*Home Truths*